DONUT LOVE

DONUT LOVE

60 Versatile Recipes for Every Kind of Craving

SLOANE PAPA

creator of Sloane's Table

PAGE STREET
PUBLISHING CO.

PAGE STREET
PUBLISHING CO.

First published in 2023 by
Page Street Publishing Co.
27 Congress Street, Suite 1511
Salem, MA 01970
www.pagestreetpublishing.com

Distributed by Macmillan, sales in Canada by The Canadian Manda Group.

27   26   25   24   23   1   2   3   4   5

ISBN-13: 978-1-64567-921-9
ISBN-10: 1-64567-921-7

Library of Congress Control Number: 2022950271

Cover and book design by Emma Hardy for Page Street Publishing Co.
Photography by Sloane Papa

Printed and bound in the United States of America

FOR MY DAD

who taught me to never shy
away from my creative dreams

TABLE OF CONTENTS

Introduction   8

Pillowy Brioche Donuts   11

Base Brioche Donut Dough   13
The Classic Trio   15
Strawberries & Cream   19
Boozy Bourbon Apple Fritters   21
The Ultimate Caramel
Movie Snack   25
Mini Boston Cream   26
Coffee Coffee Coffee   29
Mini Strawberry & Cardamom   31
Raspberry Cheesecake   35
Lemon Meringue   36
Cozy Hot Chocolate   39
Nutella Bomboloni   40

Comforting Old-Fashioned Donuts   43

Classic Sour Cream   45
Chocolate Sour Cream   46
Mini Powdered Sugar   49
Bright & Floral Lemon Lavender   51
Comfy Banana Bread   55
Mini Pumpkin Spice   56
Spiced Apple Cider   59
Zingy Ginger Molasses   61

Decadent Baked Cake Donuts   65

Coffee Coffee Cake   67
Birthday Cake   71
Mini Double Dark Chocolate   72
Melt-in-Your-Mouth Red Velvet   75
Delicate Carrot Cake   76
Caramel Coconut Rum   79
Lemon Almond Olive Oil   80
Nostalgic Cereal Milk   83
Malted Milk Chocolate   84
Marbled Neapolitan   87

Flaky Croissant Donuts 89

Base Croissant Dough 91
Creamy Dreamy Tiramisu 93
Funfetti Sprinkles & Cream 97
Apricot Earl Grey 99
Blood Orange Braids 103
White Chocolate Cappuccino 104
Ooey Gooey Turtle 107

Irresistible Choux Donuts 111

Base Choux Dough 113
Classic Vanilla Bean 114
Chocolate Chocolate Cream 117
Raspberry, Rose & Coriander 118
Chocolate Churro & Hot Chocolate 121
Dirty Chai Cream 125

Addicting Savory Donuts 127

Garlic-Herb Brioche Knots 129
Mini Cheddar Chive Croissant 131
Mini Honey–Corn Bread Old-Fashioned 135
Baked Asiago Zucchini 136
Spinach Artichoke Choux 139

Tempting Glazes, Fillings & Toppings 141

Simple Vanilla Glaze 143
Rich Chocolate Ganache 144
Cinnamon Sugar 145
Magic Chocolate Shell Coating 145
Salted Caramel Sauce 146
Silky Meringue 149
Whipped Cream 149
Tart Lemon Curd 150
Salted Caramel Popcorn 153
Fluffy Vanilla Bean Marshmallows 154
Vanilla Bean Pastry Cream 157
Cream Cheese Glaze 159

Acknowledgments 161
About the Author 162
Index 163

INTRODUCTION

Homemade donuts truly are a labor of love. The time and attention required to carefully measure, patiently proof, painstakingly laminate and cautiously deep-fry can only come from one place—love. There is no denying the fact that each type of donut usually takes dedicated time and effort. But this shouldn't hold you back from enjoying bakery-worthy donuts made from scratch. That's why the recipes in this book simplify the process and detail numerous tips and tricks, so you can re-create them in your own kitchen with confidence and ease. No matter what your skill level is and where your motivation comes from, whether it's a love for baking, eating or sharing with others, everyone should be able to spread the Donut Love.

My love of baking is why I dedicated these past few months to developing 60 donut, glaze, filling and topping recipes for this book. My passion for baking grew slowly throughout my childhood, starting with boxed mixes, of course. My sisters and I would frequently bake Funfetti cake in a Bundt™ pan and slather it with store-bought chocolate frosting. It wasn't until my dad started a gluten-free pasta business that I had my first experience with making a recipe from scratch. Together, we would test uniquely flavored gluten-free pasta dough recipes. He would crank the dough through the pasta machine, and I would hang fettuccine on wires draped across the kitchen to dry while the dogs would try to jump up and eat it. My fascination with food had really started to take root at that point. And by high school, I became an avid baker, making everything from cookies and brownies to macarons and croissants.

I love to bake for the technical process—weighing ingredients out to the exact gram, mixing batter in a gentle, precise method and deciphering how each ingredient impacts the texture and flavor of a recipe. In addition to the more scientific side, I also find the sensory experience of making donuts incredibly gratifying and therapeutic. From listening to the *slap slap slap* of brioche against the stand mixer bowl, to rolling out cold dough on a flour-covered surface and watching it transform into completely different textures and colors as it is fried or baked, making donuts from scratch is entertaining, calming and fascinating all at once.

I created each of these recipes with the simple intention to share unique and delicious donuts that people can fall in love with. Writing this book is my way of giving back to fellow avid and aspiring bakers, so they may be inspired to bake as my father inspired me when I was young. I hope that this book may teach you how to make your own donuts from scratch and, in turn, allow you to personally discover what it is about making donuts that deems them worth the labor of love.

HOW TO BAKE FROM THIS COOKBOOK

This is no ordinary donut cookbook. The recipes here go far beyond traditional fried brioche and baked cake donuts to include various shapes and sizes of old-fashioned donuts, croissant donuts, choux donuts and even savory donuts.

You'll notice not all the donut recipes have that signature round shape with a hole in the center. If we break down the main elements of a donut-enriched bread, cake or pastry that's fried or baked and has a topping, filling and/or glaze—the shape isn't a crucial factor that defines its dessert category. Donuts can come in all shapes, sizes, colors and flavors. Sweet or savory. Baked or fried.

Though all donuts are meant to be adorned with glazes, fillings and toppings, each recipe can be enjoyed thoroughly as plain, naked donuts! I am a firm believer that a baked good should be able to stand on its own, rather than rely on a glaze to taste great. Every type of donut in this book truly tastes delicious on its own, but each one becomes that much more special when paired with a glaze, filling or topping that complements its flavor and texture.

Each type of donut imparts a new experience depending on its base pastry and the flavors of its extra elements. A brioche donut can be transformed into pie (Lemon Meringue, page 36); an old-fashioned donut into the essence of the fall season (Spiced Apple Cider, page 59); a cake donut into a trip down memory lane (Nostalgic Cereal Milk, page 83); a croissant donut into a reinvented classic Italian dessert (Creamy Dreamy Tiramisu, page 93); a choux donut into a unique take on the Spanish churro (Chocolate Churro, page 121); and a savory donut into a fun appetizer or side (Garlic-Herb Brioche Knots, page 129).

The recipes in this cookbook were developed and curated with the intention of encouraging you to mix and match base recipes with any fillings and glazes your heart desires. Each recipe is written and pictured with a specific filling and/or glaze, which are my personal preferred pairings, but there is no one way to create the perfect

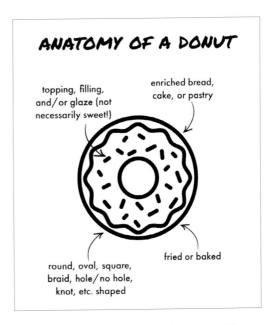

ANATOMY OF A DONUT

topping, filling, and/or glaze (not necessarily sweet!)

enriched bread, cake, or pastry

round, oval, square, braid, hole/no hole, knot, etc. shaped

fried or baked

donut. Use your creativity and explore different flavor profiles by pairing your desired donut with your favorite filling, glaze and toppings.

I challenge you to think of the donut as your blank canvas—if you could have any dessert experience, what would you create?

DONUT MISS THIS

All the recipes in this book are carefully developed with gram measurements, so you can easily re-create them in your own kitchen with success. Volume measurements are extremely inaccurate and leave room for significant errors, so your one cup of flour will differ from my one cup of flour. By providing precise measurements in grams (aside from ingredients less than 1 teaspoon), you can make these recipes accurately and with less cleanup! Trust me, once you try baking in grams, you'll never turn back!

Pillowy Brioche Donuts

These enriched golden donuts are likely the type you are most familiar with and commonly see at bakeries. With its naturally mild flavor profile, brioche may not stand out without a sweet glaze or filling. But with the right high-quality ingredients, namely unbleached all-purpose flour, large Grade AA eggs and European-style butter, a plain brioche donut warm from the deep fryer or oven should taste like a buttery dinner roll with a balanced yeasty flavor. With a blank canvas that's as delicious as this brioche, you can't go wrong with any glaze, filling or topping.

INGREDIENT STAPLES

FLOUR

The quality and type of flour greatly affects the gluten development, absorption level and taste of brioche donuts. For all the recipes in this chapter, I recommend an unbleached, all-purpose flour, such as King Arthur Baking Company® and Bob's Red Mill®, or any other high-quality flour with a protein content of 10 to 12 percent.

BUTTER

For optimal flavor and overall result, I recommend using a European-style butter, such as Kerrygold™. European-style butters have a higher fat percentage and less water content compared to American-style butters, so they tend to have the best overall flavor and consistency for baking. After all, fat equals flavor!

EQUIPMENT ESSENTIALS

| kitchen scale | electric mixer | spider skimmer | 5.5 qt dutch oven | thermometer |

It is also a general rule of thumb to use unsalted butter in order to control the total amount of salt in the recipe. You can use salted butter in any recipe, though I recommend excluding the salt listed in the recipe.

YEAST

For most baked goods, active dry and instant yeast are generally interchangeable. However, since the brioche dough requires a slow, over-night proof, I recommend using active dry yeast. If you do opt for a same day, room temperature proof, instant yeast will work just fine.

HOW TO DISPOSE OF OIL

Frying oil cannot be poured down the sink drain. The best way to dispose of oil is to let it cool completely in the pot, then pour it back into its container and throw it away in the trash.

STORING DONUTS

Brioche donuts are best enjoyed the day they are fried/baked. Freeze leftover donuts in a freezer Ziploc™ bag for up to 3 months.

Base Brioche Donut Dough

Makes 13 donuts or 18 mini donuts

Brioche is an extremely versatile yeasted bread that is enriched with milk, eggs and butter. It can be used to make a variety of baked goods, and in this case, we are of course using it to make donuts. Lean into your creative taste buds and mix and match flavors to create your own unique, bakery-worthy donuts.

FOR THE DOUGH

- 113 g (½ cup) whole milk
- 20 g (1½ tbsp) granulated sugar
- 7 g (2¼ tsp) instant or active dry yeast
- 2 eggs, room temperature
- 1 tsp vanilla bean paste or extract
- 300 g (2½ cups) all-purpose flour
- ½ tsp fine sea salt
- 85 g (6 tbsp) unsalted butter, room temperature

TO MAKE THE DOUGH: In a glass measuring cup, heat the milk to 110°F (40°C) and stir in the sugar and yeast. If using active dry yeast, allow it to sit for 15 minutes for the yeast to activate. If using instant yeast, simply move on to the next step.

Mix the eggs and vanilla into the milk-yeast mixture.

In the bowl of a stand mixer fitted with a dough hook, mix the flour and salt. Pour the wet ingredients into the flour and mix on low-medium speed for about 3 minutes, or until it forms a ball around the hook.

(continued)

BASE BRIOCHE DONUT DOUGH
(CONTINUED)

DONUT MISS THIS

All brioche donuts can be baked! Brush the egg wash of 1 egg plus 28 grams (2 tbsp) of heavy cream on the proofed donuts. Bake at 350°F (180°C) for about 10 minutes, or until an internal thermometer reads 190°F (85°C).

Add in a few pieces of butter at a time, allowing them to fully incorporate before adding more. Once all the butter is incorporated, turn the mixer up to medium-high speed and mix for 8 to 12 minutes. The dough will eventually pull away from the sides of the bowl and have a silky-smooth texture with minimal stickiness.

TO CHECK IF THE DOUGH IS READY, USE THE WINDOW-PANE TEST: Tear off a small piece and carefully spread it out to see if you can see the light through it without it tearing. Once the dough is ready, transfer it to a lightly greased bowl, cover and allow to proof overnight in the fridge. Alternatively, let the dough rise in a warm place for about 1 hour, or until doubled in size.

The next day, use the dough to make fried or baked brioche donuts.

HOW TO PROOF BRIOCHE DOUGH

Compared to croissant donuts, brioche donuts have much more yeast and a more delicate proofing window. The base dough needs to be proofed overnight for ease in handling/rolling out the cold dough, as well as more controlled proofing.

Once the dough is cut out into donuts, it should be proofed for about 30 minutes, or until nearly room temperature but still slightly cool to the touch. When pressed with a finger, the dough will slowly spring back. If it springs back quickly, it needs more time to proof; if it doesn't spring back at all, it is over-proofed.

Properly proofed brioche donuts will float in the hot oil, form a white ring around the center once fully fried, and have an even fluffy interior. Under-proofed brioche donuts will sink in the hot oil and result in a very dense interior. Over-proofed brioche donuts result in a gap between the interior and outside of the donut.

TROUBLESHOOTING OVER-PROOFED BRIOCHE: If your oil is taking longer to heat up than expected, you can always place the donuts back in the fridge to slow down the yeast before they over-proof. If they're already over-proofed, go ahead and fry them as quickly as possible. They won't be perfect, but they'll still taste great!

THE CLASSIC TRIO

Makes 13 donuts

If I'm making a donut run for a Sunday morning treat, you can bet it will be a baker's dozen of three types of donuts: chocolate sprinkle, cinnamon sugar and plain ol' glazed. These timeless flavors are so simple, which is exactly why they can be the trickiest to perfect. My version of a chocolate sprinkle donut has a rich chocolate ganache that's so thick after just one bite you'll be smiling with chocolate-coated teeth. My cinnamon sugar donut has the ideal sugar-to-cinnamon ratio reminiscent of cinnamon sugar toast, and my glazed donut shines from its sweet, glassy sheen that shatters with each bite.

FOR THE DOUGH

- 1 batch Base Brioche Donut Dough (page 13)

FOR FRYING THE DONUTS

- 48–64 oz (1½–2 quarts) neutral oil

TO FRY THE DONUTS: About 30 minutes before rolling out the dough, fill a Dutch oven or heavy-bottomed pot with enough neutral oil to cover 2 inches (5 cm). Place the oil over medium heat and bring it to 355°F (180°C).

Place a wire rack over a paper towel–lined baking sheet. On a separate baking sheet, cut out thirteen 4-inch (10-cm) parchment squares for the donuts.

On a lightly floured surface, roll the dough out to ½ inch (1.3 cm) in thickness. Brush away any excess flour. Use well-floured 3-inch (8-cm) and 1-inch (2.5-cm) round cutters to cut out as many donuts as possible and place each on a parchment square. Shape the excess dough into a disk, then wrap it in plastic wrap and chill for at least 15 minutes before re-rolling and cutting out more donuts.

Cover the donuts and allow them to rise for about 30 minutes, or until nearly room temperature but still slightly cool to the touch. When pressed with a finger, the dough will slowly spring back.

The Classic Trio
(CONTINUED)

FOR THE GLAZE/COATING
- ½ batch Thin Vanilla Glaze (page 143)
- ½ batch Cinnamon Sugar (page 145)
- ½ batch Rich Chocolate Ganache (page 144)
- Chocolate sprinkles, for topping

Meanwhile, make the vanilla glaze, cinnamon sugar, or chocolate ganache.

Once proofed, use the parchment squares to gently lower two to three donuts into the hot oil. Fry the donuts for 90 seconds on the first side, then flip over and fry for 90 seconds until golden. Transfer the donuts to the wire rack. Wait a couple minutes for the oil to come back up to 355°F (180°C), then continue frying the donuts.

TO GLAZE WITH THE VANILLA GLAZE: Once the donuts have cooled just enough to handle, dip four or five donuts in the vanilla glaze.

TO COAT WITH THE CINNAMON SUGAR: Once the donuts have cooled just enough to handle, toss four or five donuts in the cinnamon sugar.

TO GLAZE WITH CHOCOLATE GANACHE: Once the donuts have cooled completely, make the ganache, then dip four or five donuts and top them with chocolate sprinkles.

STRAWBERRIES & CREAM

Makes 12 donuts

The pairing of fresh strawberries and whipped cream is so simple, yet so magical. Some of my fondest early food memories involve sneaking some strawberries from the fridge and dunking them into a large tub of Cool Whip®—with a hefty Cool Whip to strawberry ratio, of course. As a kid, everything from the sweet, juicy fruit to the matte, velvety mouthfeel of the whipped cream represented pure joy. So, these heart donuts inspired by strawberry-and-cream are an ode to the love for the simplest things that bring us so much joy.

FOR THE DOUGH

- 1 batch Base Brioche Donut Dough (page 13)

FOR FRYING THE DONUTS

- 48–64 oz (1½–2 quarts) neutral oil

TO FRY THE DONUTS: About 30 minutes before rolling out the dough, fill a Dutch oven or heavy-bottomed pot with enough neutral oil to cover 2 inches (5 cm). Place the oil over medium heat and bring it to 355°F (180°C).

Place a wire rack over a paper towel-lined baking sheet. On a separate baking sheet, cut out twelve 4-inch (10-cm) parchment squares for the donuts.

On a lightly floured surface, roll the dough out to ½ inch (1.3 cm) in thickness. Brush away any excess flour. Use a well-floured 3-inch (8-cm) heart-shaped cutter to cut out as many donuts as possible and place each on a parchment square. Shape the excess dough into a disk, then wrap it in plastic wrap and chill for at least 15 minutes before rerolling and cutting out more donuts.

Cover the donuts and allow them to rise for about 30 minutes, or until nearly room temperature but still slightly cool to the touch. When pressed with a finger, the dough will slowly spring back.

Once proofed, use the parchment squares to gently lower two to three donuts into the hot oil. Fry the donuts for 2 minutes on the first side, then flip over and fry for 2 minutes until golden. Transfer the donuts to the wire rack. Wait a couple minutes for the oil to come back up to 355°F (180°C), then continue frying the donuts.

(continued)

STRAWBERRIES + CREAM
(CONTINUED)

FOR THE COATING, FILLING + TOPPING

- 100 g (½ cup) granulated sugar
- 1 batch Strawberry Pastry Cream (page 158)
- 1 batch Whipped Cream (page 149)
- 6 fresh strawberries, sliced in half

TO GLAZE: Once the donuts have cooled just enough to handle, toss them in the sugar.

TO FILL: Transfer the strawberry pastry cream and whipped cream to piping bags with small round piping tips. Use a long skewer to poke a hole into each donut, pushing it almost all the way through the other side.

Pipe the pastry cream into each donut, then top them with whipped cream. Top each with a strawberry half.

DONUT MISS THIS

Before starting a recipe, read the ingredients and instructions all the way through twice. Homemade donuts are not inherently easy to make, but I have packed each recipe with carefully worded instructions and tips so you can re-create bakery-quality donuts with ease in your own kitchen. To minimize kitchen chaos, read through the recipe thoroughly and digest the information by visualizing yourself making it in your kitchen. Ask yourself: Do I have all the necessary ingredients/tools? Is there room in the fridge to chill the croissant donuts on several baking sheets?

Then, plan out which elements need to be made the night before. Does the dough need to rise overnight? Do you want to make the pastry cream the day before to save time? Furthermore, pay close attention to the timing of each element the day of frying the donuts, such as when to start heating up the oil; how long the donuts need to proof; if you need a glaze/coating ready to use immediately after the donuts have been fried.

Walking through these steps in your head in the context of your own kitchen prior to starting the recipe will help everything flow smoothly, so you can truly enjoy the process of baking.

Boozy Bourbon Apple Fritters

Makes 9 donuts

While some apple fritters are made with a thin, cake-like batter, these bakery-style fritters are made with brioche and precooked apple filling. The spiced apples tucked away into a soft, neutral dough create an irresistible apple pie situation. Now maybe it's just me, but apple fritters have always felt like a grown-up type of donut, so what better way to make this recipe a bit more mature than by submerging them in a boozy bourbon glaze. What I love about this glaze is that it repurposes the sauce from the apple filling, giving it a warm, spiced apple flavor married with your favorite bourbon.

FOR THE DOUGH

- 1 batch Base Brioche Donut Dough (page 13)

FOR THE SPICED APPLES

- 300 g (about 2) Honeycrisp apples, peeled and cut into small cubes
- 15 g (1 tbsp) lemon juice
- 106 g (½ cup, packed) dark brown sugar
- 1 tsp ground cinnamon
- ¼ tsp ground allspice
- ¼ tsp ground nutmeg
- ¼ tsp ground cloves
- ¼ tsp ground ginger
- ¼ tsp ground cardamom
- 1 tsp vanilla extract
- 12 g (1 tbsp) bourbon
- 28 g (2 tbsp) unsalted butter
- 15 g (2 tbsp) all-purpose flour

TO MAKE THE SPICED APPLES: In a large bowl, toss together the apples, lemon juice, brown sugar, cinnamon, allspice, nutmeg, cloves, ginger, cardamom, vanilla and bourbon.

Place a large skillet over medium heat. Add the butter, stirring frequently with a rubber spatula until the milk solids have separated and darkened.

Add the apples and stir frequently for about 4 to 5 minutes until they have softened. Stir in the flour and continue to cook for 2 to 3 minutes until the liquid has thickened. Remove it from the heat.

On a small baking sheet, spread the apples in an even layer and allow them to cool completely. Alternatively, you can make the spiced apples the day before when you make the brioche, and chill them overnight.

(continued)

Boozy Bourbon Apple Fritters

(CONTINUED)

FOR FRYING THE DONUTS

- 48–64 oz (1½–2 quarts) neutral oil

FOR THE GLAZE

- 170 g (1½ cups) confectioners' sugar
- 42 g (3 tbsp) apple filling sauce, leftover after apples are added to the dough
- 24 g (2 tbsp) bourbon

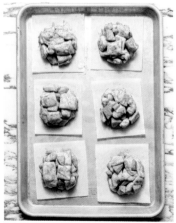

TO FRY THE DONUTS: About 30 minutes before rolling out the dough, fill a Dutch oven or heavy-bottomed pot with enough neutral oil to cover 2 inches (5 cm). Place the oil over medium heat and bring it to 355°F (180°C).

Place a wire rack over a paper towel-lined baking sheet. On a separate baking sheet, cut out nine 4-inch (10-cm) parchment squares for the donuts.

On a lightly floured surface, roll the dough out to ¼ inch (6 mm) in thickness. Dust the dough with some extra flour. Reserving most of the sauce, use a fork to add the apples to half of the dough. Dust the apples with more flour, then fold the other half of the dough over on top. Using a bench scraper or large knife, cut the dough into 1-inch (2.5-cm) pieces. Use your hands to gently toss the pieces to separate.

Divide the pieces into nine portions, weighing about 100 grams each. Squish the portions in your hands so the brioche pieces adhere to each other. Place each on a parchment square and pat them down to no more than 1 inch (2.5 cm) in thickness.

Cover the donuts and allow them to rise for about 30 minutes, or until nearly room temperature but still slightly cool to the touch. When pressed with a finger, the dough will slowly spring back.

MEANWHILE, MAKE THE BOURBON GLAZE: In a small bowl, whisk together the confectioners' sugar, reserved apple filling sauce and bourbon until smooth.

Once proofed, give the fritters one final squeeze to ensure they stick together, then use the parchment squares to gently lower two to three donuts into the hot oil. Fry the donuts for 2½ minutes on the first side, then flip over and fry for 2½ minutes until golden. Transfer the donuts to the wire rack. Wait a couple minutes for the oil to come back up to 355°F (180°C), then continue frying the donuts.

TO GLAZE: Once the donuts have cooled just enough to handle, dip them in the glaze.

THE ULTIMATE
CARAMEL MOVIE SNACK

Makes 13 donuts

Microwave popcorn is one of my movie snack guilty pleasures. I love everything, from the sound of the *pop pop pop* as it rotates in the microwave to the way that the corners of the bag are gently pulled apart to let out buttery steam. I *live* for that last one. While microwave popcorn will always have a special place in my heart, these donuts supersede it on all fronts. The popcorn is upleveled with the most addicting salted caramel candy coating, and rather than a noisy paper bag, its container is a soft brioche donut dunked in a brown butter caramel sauce.

FOR THE DOUGH

- 1 batch Base Brioche Donut Dough (page 13)

FOR FRYING THE DONUTS

- 48–64 oz (1½–2 quarts) neutral oil

FOR THE GLAZE + TOPPING

- 1 batch Brown Butter Caramel Sauce (page 146)
- 1 batch Salted Caramel Popcorn (page 153)

TO FRY THE DONUTS: About 30 minutes before rolling out the dough, fill a Dutch oven or heavy-bottomed pot with enough neutral oil to cover 2 inches (5 cm). Place the oil over medium heat and bring it to 355°F (180°C).

Place a wire rack over a paper towel-lined baking sheet. On a separate baking sheet, cut out thirteen 4-inch (10-cm) parchment squares for the donuts.

On a lightly floured surface, roll the dough out to ½ inch (1.3 cm) in thickness. Brush away any excess flour. Use well-floured 3-inch (8-cm) and 1-inch (2.5-cm) round cutters to cut out as many donuts as possible and place each on a parchment square. Shape the excess dough into a disk, then wrap it in plastic wrap and chill for at least 15 minutes before rerolling and cutting out more donuts.

Cover the donuts and allow them to rise for about 30 minutes, or until nearly room temperature but still slightly cool to the touch. When pressed with a finger, the dough will slowly spring back.

Once proofed, use the parchment squares to gently lower two to three donuts into the hot oil. Fry the donuts for 90 seconds on the first side, then flip over and fry for 90 seconds until golden. Transfer the donuts to the wire rack. Wait a couple minutes for the oil to come back up to 355°F (180°C), then continue frying the donuts.

TO GLAZE: Once the donuts have cooled just enough to handle, dip each one in the caramel sauce and top it with salted caramel popcorn.

Mini Boston Cream

Makes 16 mini donuts

Boston Cream is another classic donut that I couldn't pass up. They aren't so decadent that you can only eat a few bites; they're just decadent enough that you want to eat the whole batch. So, rather than testing your self-control, let's share the donut love. This miniature version makes two to three bite pastries that are ideal for giving away or bringing to dinner parties.

FOR THE DOUGH

- 1 batch Base Brioche Donut Dough (page 13)

FOR FRYING THE DONUTS

- 48–64 oz (1½–2 quarts) neutral oil

FOR THE COATING + FILLING

- 1 batch Vanilla Bean Pastry Cream (page 157)
- ½ batch Rich Chocolate Ganache (page 144)

DONUT MISS THIS

Take the exact time written with a grain of salt. Just as we have established that your one cup of flour will be different from mine, it is safe to say that there are even more variables when it comes to our electric mixers, stoves and ovens. Please keep the times as a guideline, and focus more on the visual doneness indicators, such as "until deeply golden" or "until a toothpick inserted comes out clean."

TO FRY THE DONUTS: About 30 minutes before rolling out the dough, fill a Dutch oven or heavy-bottomed pot with enough neutral oil to cover 2 inches (5 cm). Place the oil over medium heat and bring it to 355°F (180°C).

Place a wire rack over a paper towel-lined baking sheet. On a separate baking sheet, cut out sixteen 3-inch (8-cm) parchment squares for the donuts.

On a lightly floured surface, roll the dough out to ½ inch (1.25 cm) in thickness. Brush away any excess flour. Use a well-floured 2-inch (5-cm) round cutter to cut out as many donuts as possible and place each on a parchment square. Shape the excess dough into a disk, then wrap it in plastic wrap and chill for at least 15 minutes before rerolling and cutting out more donuts.

Cover the donuts and allow them to rise for about 30 minutes, or until nearly room temperature but still slightly cool to the touch. When pressed with a finger, the dough will slowly spring back.

Once proofed, use the parchment squares to gently lower two to three donuts into the hot oil. Fry the donuts for 90 seconds on the first side, then flip over and fry for 90 seconds until golden. Transfer the donuts to the wire rack to cool completely. Wait a couple minutes for the oil to come back up to 355°F (180°C), then continue frying the donuts.

TO FILL AND GLAZE: Transfer the vanilla bean pastry cream to a piping bag with a small round piping tip. Use a long skewer to poke a hole into each donut, pushing it almost all the way through the other side. Fill each donut with the pastry cream. Dip each of them in the ganache and allow to set.

COFFEE COFFEE COFFEE

Makes 6 donut braids

If you said this title in your head as fast as you could like a jittery coffee fanatic, then I'm guessing you're a coffee lover like me. And we've already established you're a donut lover, so it only makes sense that you want to make coffee-flavored donuts! Now, the braided shape was inspired by the glazed crullers from Lou's, a beloved restaurant and bakery in Hanover, New Hampshire. These crullers are actually braided brioche donuts, not choux donuts, and just like the rest of their baked goods, they were a contributing factor to my fascination with baking.

FOR THE DOUGH

- 1 batch Base Brioche Donut Dough (page 13)

FOR FRYING THE DONUTS

- 48–64 oz (1½–2 quarts) neutral oil

TO FRY THE DONUTS: About 30 minutes before rolling out the dough, fill a Dutch oven or heavy-bottomed pot with enough neutral oil to cover 2 inches (5 cm). Place the oil over medium heat and bring it to 355°F (180°C).

Place a wire rack over a paper towel-lined baking sheet. On a separate baking sheet, cut out six 6 × 3–inch (15 cm × 8–cm) parchment rectangles for the donut braids.

On a lightly floured surface, roll the dough out to ¼ inch (6 mm) in thickness. Brush away any excess flour. Use a pastry or pizza cutter to cut 1 × 5–inch (2.5 cm × 13–cm) strips. Take three strips and braid them, using a few dabs of water to help the ends stick together. Place each braid on a parchment rectangle.

Cover the donuts and allow them to rise for about 30 minutes, or until nearly room temperature but still slightly cool to the touch. When pressed with a finger, the dough will slowly spring back.

Meanwhile, make the espresso swirled glaze or espresso-cinnamon sugar.

(continued)

COFFEE COFFEE COFFEE

(CONTINUED)

FOR THE COATING/GLAZE

- ½ batch Espresso Swirled Glaze (page 143)
- ½ batch Espresso-Cinnamon Sugar (page 145)
- ½ batch Mocha Ganache (page 144)

Once proofed, use the parchment squares to gently lower two to three donuts into the hot oil. Fry the donuts for 2 minutes on the first side, then flip over and fry for 2 minutes until golden. Transfer the donuts to the wire rack. Wait a couple minutes for the oil to come back up to 355°F (180°C), then continue frying the donuts.

TO GLAZE WITH THE ESPRESSO SWIRLED GLAZE: Once the donuts have cooled just enough to handle, dip two braids in the espresso swirled glaze.

TO COAT WITH THE ESPRESSO-CINNAMON SUGAR: Once the donuts have cooled just enough to handle, toss two braids in the espresso-cinnamon sugar.

TO GLAZE WITH THE MOCHA GANACHE: Once the donuts have cooled completely, make the ganache, then dip two braids and place them back on the wire rack to set.

Mini Strawberry & Cardamom

Makes 18 mini donuts

Cardamom is one of my favorite spices to add to baked goods; its earthy undertones give it an almost calming effect. In these donuts, its unique flavor is complemented by the sweet, concentrated strawberry in both the dough and the coating. I highly recommend saving some of the homemade strawberry milk to enjoy with these!

FOR THE HOMEMADE STRAWBERRY MILK

- 85 g (½ cup) fresh strawberries, hulled and quartered
- 18 g (3 tbsp) freeze-dried strawberry powder
- 50 g (¼ cup) granulated sugar
- 56 g (¼ cup) water
- 227 g (1 cup) whole milk

FOR THE DOUGH

- 113 g (½ cup) homemade strawberry milk
- 20 g (1½ tbsp) granulated sugar
- 7 g (2¼ tsp) instant or active dry yeast
- 2 eggs, room temperature
- 1 tsp vanilla bean paste or extract
- 300 g (2½ cups) all-purpose flour
- ½ tsp fine sea salt
- 1 tsp ground cardamom
- 85 g (6 tbsp) unsalted butter, room temperature

TO MAKE THE STRAWBERRY MILK: In a small saucepan, combine the fresh strawberries, freeze-dried strawberry powder, sugar and water. Place it over medium heat, stirring frequently, for about 10 to 12 minutes until the strawberries have broken down.

Use an immersion blender or transfer to a blender, and blend until smooth. Pour the milk into the syrup and mix to combine.

Weigh 113 g (½ cup) of the strawberry milk out for the dough recipe and pour the remainder into a glass jar. Store the leftover strawberry milk in the fridge to enjoy with your donuts later!

TO MAKE THE DOUGH: In a glass measuring cup, heat the strawberry milk to 110°F (40°C) and stir in the sugar and yeast. If using active dry yeast, allow it to sit for 15 minutes for the yeast to activate. If using instant yeast, simply move on to the next step.

Mix the eggs and vanilla into the milk-yeast mixture.

In the bowl of a stand mixer fitted with a dough hook, mix the flour, salt and cardamom. Pour the wet ingredients into the flour and mix on low-medium speed for about 3 minutes, or until it forms a ball around the hook.

Add in a few pieces of butter at a time, allowing them to fully incorporate before adding more. Once all the butter is incorporated, turn the mixer up to medium-high speed and mix for 8 to 12 minutes. The dough will eventually pull away from the sides of the bowl and have a silky-smooth texture with minimal stickiness.

(continued)

Mini Strawberry + Cardamom

(CONTINUED)

FOR FRYING THE DONUTS

- 48–64 oz (1½–2 quarts) neutral oil

FOR THE COATING

- 100 g (½ cup) granulated sugar
- 12 g (2 tbsp) freeze-dried strawberry powder
- 1 tsp ground cardamom

USE THE WINDOWPANE TEST: Tear off a small piece and carefully spread it out to see if you can see the light through it without it tearing. Once the dough is ready, transfer it to a lightly greased bowl, cover and allow to proof overnight in the fridge. Alternatively, let the dough rise in a warm place for about 1 hour, or until doubled in size.

TO FRY THE DONUTS: About 30 minutes before rolling out the dough, fill a Dutch oven or heavy-bottomed pot with enough neutral oil to cover 2 inches (5 cm). Place the oil over medium heat and bring it to 355°F (180°C).

Place a wire rack over a paper towel-lined baking sheet. On a separate baking sheet, cut out eighteen 3-inch (8-cm) parchment squares for the donuts.

On a lightly floured surface, roll the dough out to ½ inch (1.3 cm) in thickness. Brush away any excess flour. Use well-floured 2-inch (5-cm) and ½-inch (1.3-cm) round cutters to cut out as many donuts as possible and place each on a parchment square. Shape the excess dough into a disk, then wrap it in plastic wrap and chill for at least 15 minutes before rerolling and cutting out more donuts.

Cover the donuts and allow them to rise for about 30 minutes, or until nearly room temperature but still slightly cool to the touch. When pressed with a finger, the dough will slowly spring back.

Once proofed, use the parchment squares to gently lower two to three donuts into the hot oil. Fry the donuts for 75 seconds on the first side, then flip over and fry for 75 seconds until golden. Transfer the donuts to the wire rack. Wait a couple minutes for the oil to come back up to 355°F (180°C), then continue frying the donuts.

MEANWHILE, MAKE THE COATING: In a medium bowl, combine the sugar, freeze-dried strawberry powder and cardamom. Once the donuts have cooled just enough to handle, toss them in the strawberry-cardamom sugar.

RASPBERRY CHEESECAKE

Makes 12 donuts

I couldn't write a whole donut book and not include a classic, jelly-filled, confectioners' sugar donut. Buuuut I also couldn't not elevate it. So, I bring to you these raspberry cheesecake brioche donuts, featuring a Cream Cheese Pastry Cream (page 158), sweet raspberry jam and a generous coating of confectioners' sugar.

FOR THE DOUGH
- 1 batch Base Brioche Donut Dough (page 13)

FOR FRYING THE DONUTS
- 48–64 oz (1½–2 quarts) neutral oil

FOR THE COATING, FILLING + TOPPING
- 170 g (½ cup) raspberry jam
- 113 g (1 cup) confectioners' sugar
- 1 batch Cream Cheese Pastry Cream (page 158)
- Fresh raspberries, for topping

TO FRY THE DONUTS: About 30 minutes before rolling out the dough, fill a Dutch oven or heavy-bottomed pot with enough neutral oil to cover 2 inches (5 cm). Place the oil over medium heat and bring it to 355°F (180°C).

Place a wire rack over a paper towel-lined baking sheet. On a separate baking sheet, cut out twelve 4-inch (10-cm) parchment squares for the donuts.

On a lightly floured surface, roll the dough out to ½ inch (1.3 cm) in thickness. Brush away any excess flour. Use a well-floured 3-inch (8-cm) round cutter to cut out as many donuts as possible and place each on a parchment square. Shape the excess dough into a disk, then wrap it in plastic wrap and chill for at least 15 minutes before rerolling and cutting out more donuts.

Cover the donuts and allow them to rise for about 30 minutes, or until nearly room temperature but still slightly cool to the touch. When pressed with a finger, the dough will slowly spring back.

Once proofed, use the parchment squares to gently lower two to three donuts into the hot oil. Fry the donuts for 2½ minutes on the first side, then flip over and fry for 2½ minutes until golden. Transfer the donuts to the wire rack to cool completely. Wait a couple minutes for the oil to come back up to 355°F (180°C), then continue frying the donuts.

TO ASSEMBLE: Transfer the raspberry jam to a piping bag and transfer the pastry cream to a piping bag with a small round piping tip. Use a long skewer to poke a hole into each donut, almost through to the other side.

Toss each cooled donut in confectioners' sugar. Pipe a small amount of raspberry jam into each donut. Then, fill them with the pastry cream. Top each one with a fresh raspberry.

LEMON MERINGUE

Makes 10 donuts

There's just something so fun about donuts tasting like another dessert. By filling these long, oval, fried brioche donuts with a sweet-and-tart lemon curd (page 150) and decorating them with a meringue topping (page 149), they create such a unique (not to mention delicious) pie-donut fusion!

FOR THE DOUGH

- 1 batch Base Brioche Donut Dough (page 13)

FOR FRYING THE DONUTS

- 48–64 oz (1½–2 quarts) neutral oil

FOR THE FILLING + TOPPING

- 1 batch Tart Lemon Curd (page 150)
- 1 batch Silky Meringue (page 149)

DONUT BREAK

A note on separating eggs: This is a contentious topic among avid bakers, and of course I do have a strong opinion on it. The best way to separate an egg is by cracking a cold egg into a shallow bowl. With clean hands, gently pluck the egg yolk from the whites. As you hold the yolk in your hand, gravity will pull the whites away from the yolk and they will fall back into the bowl.

TO FRY THE DONUTS: About 30 minutes before rolling out the dough, fill a Dutch oven or heavy-bottomed pot with enough neutral oil to cover 2 inches (5 cm). Place the oil over medium heat and bring it to 355°F (180°C).

Place a wire rack over a paper towel-lined baking sheet. On a separate baking sheet, cut out ten 6 × 2–inch (15 cm × 5–cm) parchment rectangles for the donuts.

On a lightly floured surface, roll the dough out to ½ inch (1.3 cm) in thickness. Brush away any excess flour. Use a well-floured 5 × 1.5–inch (13 cm × 4–cm) oval cutter to cut out as many donuts as possible and place each on a parchment rectangle. Shape the excess dough into a disk, then wrap it in plastic wrap and chill for at least 15 minutes before rerolling and cutting out more donuts.

Cover the donuts and allow them to rise for about 30 minutes, or until nearly room temperature but still slightly cool to the touch. When pressed with a finger, the dough will slowly spring back.

Once proofed, use the parchment squares to gently lower two to three donuts into the hot oil. Fry the donuts for 2½ minutes on the first side, then flip over and fry for 2½ minutes until golden. Transfer the donuts to the wire rack to cool. Wait a couple minutes for the oil to come back up to 355°F (180°C), then continue frying the donuts.

TO FILL: Transfer the lemon curd to a piping bag with a small round piping tip. Use a long skewer to poke a hole into one short side of each donut, pushing it almost all the way through the other side. Pipe the lemon curd into them until you feel resistance.

TO PIPE MERINGUE: Transfer the meringue to a piping bag with a small petal tip. Pipe the meringue on top of each donut, and use a kitchen torch to give a little color, if desired.

COZY HOT CHOCOLATE

Makes 12 donuts

Nothing could possibly be better on a crisp winter night than a steaming cup of rich hot chocolate with mini marshmallows melting into a thick layer of frothy sweetness—unless it's all wrapped up into a pillowy-soft, golden brioche donut.

FOR THE DOUGH

- 1 batch Base Brioche Donut Dough (page 13)

FOR FRYING THE DONUTS

- 48–64 oz (1½–2 quarts) neutral oil

FOR THE COATING, FILLING + TOPPING

- 100 g (½ cup) granulated sugar
- 1 batch Rich Chocolate Ganache (page 144)
- 1 batch Fluffy Vanilla Bean Marshmallows (page 154)

TO FRY THE DONUTS: About 30 minutes before rolling out the dough, fill a Dutch oven or heavy-bottomed pot with enough neutral oil to cover 2 inches (5 cm). Place the oil over medium heat and bring it to 355°F (180°C).

Place a wire rack over a paper towel-lined baking sheet. On a separate baking sheet, cut out twelve 4-inch (10-cm) parchment squares for the donuts.

On a lightly floured surface, roll the dough out to ½ inch (1.3 cm) in thickness. Brush away any excess flour. Use a well-floured 3-inch (8-cm) round cutter to cut out as many donuts as possible and place each on a parchment square. Shape the excess dough into a disk, then wrap it in plastic wrap and chill for at least 15 minutes before rerolling and cutting out more donuts.

Cover the donuts and allow them to rise for about 30 minutes, or until nearly room temperature but still slightly cool to the touch. When pressed with a finger, the dough will slowly spring back.

Once proofed, use the parchment squares to gently lower two to three donuts into the hot oil. Fry the donuts for 2½ minutes on the first side, then flip over and fry for 2½ minutes until golden. Transfer the donuts to the wire rack. Once they've cooled just enough to handle, toss them in the sugar. Wait a couple minutes for the oil to come back up to 355°F (180°C), then continue frying the donuts.

TO FILL: Transfer the chocolate ganache to a piping bag with a small round piping tip. Use a long skewer to poke a hole into each donut, pushing it almost all the way through the other side. Pipe the ganache into each donut. Top each donut with a marshmallow.

Nutella Bomboloni

Makes 12 donuts

This recipe resembles traditional bomboloni in the way that it uses an enriched dough flavored with orange zest, fried into golden pillows and filled from the top rather than the side. The hint of citrus complements the chocolate hazelnut filling to create the most delicious Italian pastry–inspired donut.

. . . .

FOR THE DOUGH

- 1 batch Base Brioche Donut Dough (page 13)
- Zest of 1 orange

FOR FRYING THE DONUTS

- 48–64 oz (1½–2 quarts) neutral oil

FOR THE COATING + FILLING

- 100 g (½ cup) granulated sugar
- 150 g (½ cup) chocolate hazelnut spread, such as Nutella®

TO MAKE THE DOUGH: Follow the Base Brioche Donut Dough recipe (page 13) as written, but add the zest of one orange to the dry ingredients.

TO FRY THE DONUTS: About 30 minutes before rolling out the dough, fill a Dutch oven or heavy-bottomed pot with enough neutral oil to cover 2 inches (5 cm). Place the oil over medium heat and bring it to 355°F (180°C).

Place a wire rack over a paper towel–lined baking sheet. On a separate baking sheet, cut out twelve 4-inch (10-cm) parchment squares for the donuts.

On a lightly floured surface, roll the dough out to ½ inch (1.3 cm) in thickness. Brush away any excess flour. Use a well-floured 3-inch (8-cm) round cutter to cut out as many donuts as possible and place each on a parchment square. Shape the excess dough into a disk, then wrap it in plastic wrap and chill for at least 15 minutes before rerolling and cutting out more donuts.

Cover the donuts and allow them to rise for about 30 minutes, or until nearly room temperature but still slightly cool to the touch. When pressed with a finger, the dough will slowly spring back.

Once proofed, use the parchment squares to gently lower two to three donuts into the hot oil. Fry the donuts for 2½ minutes on the first side, then flip over and fry for 2½ minutes until golden. Transfer the donuts to the wire rack. Once they've cooled just enough to handle, toss them in the sugar. Wait a couple minutes for the oil to come back up to 355°F (180°C), then continue frying the donuts.

TO FILL: Transfer the chocolate hazelnut spread to a piping bag with a small round piping tip. Use a long skewer to poke a hole into the top of each donut, almost through to the other side. Pipe the filling into each donut.

COMFORTING OLD-FASHIONED DONUTS

One of the many magical things about donuts is that they can be dressed up or down. As their name suggests, old-fashioned donuts are ideal for the commonly beloved flavors, such as vanilla, chocolate and lemon. These fried cake donuts maintain a soft and fluffy interior from high-quality cake flour, large Grade AA eggs and a gentle technique to roll out the dough to avoid overdeveloping the gluten. Flavors fit for fall and winter seasons, like banana bread, apple cider, pumpkin spice and ginger molasses all allow the soft interior to shine and add an extra level of comfort.

INGREDIENT STAPLES

FLOUR

All old-fashioned donut recipes are made with cake flour to achieve the softest crumb possible, despite being worked a moderate amount from rolling out, cutting and rolling out again. A high-quality and common brand for cake flour is Swan's Down®. Alternatively, you can make a DIY version by using all-purpose flour, taking out 15 grams (2 tbsp) and adding in 16 grams (2 tbsp) of cornstarch.

CHEMICAL LEAVENING AGENTS

Chemical leaveners, primarily baking powder and baking soda, are essential to old-fashioned donuts' rise and texture. These leaveners lose their power over time, so if you don't bake often enough to go through them quickly, check their freshness before using. For baking powder, test

EQUIPMENT ESSENTIALS

kitchen scale · electric mixer · spider skimmer · 5.5 qt dutch oven · thermometer

a small amount in some water; and for baking soda, test a small amount in some vinegar. If they foam, you're good to go!

SOUR CREAM & YOGURT

In all recipes, sour cream and yogurt are interchangeable. I recommend baking only with plain, whole-milk Greek yogurt or a yogurt similar in consistency to Greek, such as Icelandic. The whole-milk fat content and thick consistency are ideal for best overall flavor and texture of baked goods. The same goes for sour cream in terms of fat content.

HOW TO DISPOSE OF OIL

Frying oil cannot be poured down the sink drain. The best way to dispose of oil is to let it cool completely in the pot, then pour it back into its container and throw it away in the trash.

STORING DONUTS

Old-fashioned donuts are best enjoyed the day they are fried. Freeze leftover donuts in a freezer Ziploc bag for up to 3 months.

CLASSIC SOUR CREAM

Makes 13 donuts

If homemade old-fashioned donuts have been on your baking to-do list, then this is the perfect recipe to start with. These have a bit of nutmeg, a spice that's hard to put your finger on at first, but adds a level of warmth and depth of flavor that truly sets these donuts apart from the rest.

FOR THE DOUGH

- 300 g (2½ cups) cake flour
- 6 g (1½ tsp) baking powder
- ¼ tsp baking soda
- ½ tsp fine sea salt
- ½ tsp ground nutmeg
- 56 g (¼ cup) unsalted butter, room temperature
- 150 g (¾ cup) granulated sugar
- 1 egg, room temperature
- 1 tsp vanilla bean paste
- 170 g (¾ cup) sour cream, room temperature

FOR FRYING THE DONUTS

- 48–64 oz (1½–2 quarts) vegetable oil

FOR THE GLAZE

- 1 batch Thin Vanilla Glaze (page 143)

TO MAKE THE DOUGH: In a large bowl, combine the flour, baking powder, baking soda, salt and nutmeg. Set it aside.

In the bowl of a stand mixer fitted with the paddle attachment, cream the butter and sugar for 2 to 3 minutes until light and fluffy. Mix in the egg and vanilla until fully combined.

Scrape down the bowl and add half of the dry ingredients. Mix on low speed until barely combined, then mix in the sour cream. Add the rest of the dry ingredients, and mix until just combined. Cover the bowl and place it in the fridge to chill for at least 1 hour or overnight.

TO FRY THE DONUTS: Just before rolling out the dough, fill a Dutch oven or heavy-bottomed pot with enough vegetable oil to cover 2 inches (5 cm). Heat the oil over low-medium heat and bring it to 350°F (180°C).

Place a wire rack over a paper towel–lined baking sheet. On a separate baking sheet, cut out thirteen 4-inch (10-cm) parchment squares for the donuts.

Roll the dough out between two pieces of well-floured parchment paper to ½ inch (1.3 cm) in thickness. Brush away any excess flour. Use well-floured 3-inch (8-cm) and 1-inch (2.5-cm) round cutters to cut out as many donuts as possible and place each on a parchment square. Reroll the dough and cut out more donuts as needed.

Use the parchment squares to gently lower two to three donuts into the hot oil. Fry the donuts for 3 minutes on the first side, then flip over and fry for 2 minutes until golden. Transfer the donuts to the wire rack. Wait a couple minutes for the oil to come back up to 350°F (180°C), then continue frying the donuts.

TO GLAZE: Once the donuts have cooled just enough to handle, dip them in the vanilla glaze.

CHOCOLATE SOUR CREAM

Makes 13 donuts

As someone with a major sweet tooth, I have of course always loved chocolate. And something not quite as common among bakers, I *love* sour cream. Eat it by the spoonful kind of love. Anyway . . . these two magical ingredients have been brought together in this recipe to create the most tender, moist and chocolatey old-fashioned donuts, reminiscent of cookies and cream!

FOR THE DOUGH

- 270 g (2¼ cups) cake flour
- 42 g (½ cup) Dutch process cocoa powder
- 21 g (¼ cup) black cocoa powder
- 6 g (1½ tsp) baking powder
- ¼ tsp baking soda
- ½ tsp fine sea salt
- 56 g (¼ cup) unsalted butter, room temperature
- 150 g (¾ cup) granulated sugar
- 1 egg, room temperature
- 1 tsp vanilla bean paste
- 170 g (¾ cup) sour cream, room temperature

FOR FRYING THE DONUTS

- 48–64 oz (1½–2 quarts) vegetable oil

FOR THE GLAZE

- 1 batch Thin Vanilla Glaze (page 143)

TO MAKE THE DOUGH: In a large bowl, combine the flour, cocoa powders, baking powder, baking soda and salt. Set it aside.

In the bowl of a stand mixer fitted with the paddle attachment, cream the butter and sugar for 2 to 3 minutes until light and fluffy. Mix in the egg and vanilla until fully combined.

Scrape down the bowl and add half of the dry ingredients. Mix on low speed until barely combined, then mix in the sour cream. Add the rest of the dry ingredients, and mix until just combined. Cover the bowl and place it in the fridge to chill for at least 1 hour or overnight.

TO FRY THE DONUTS: Just before rolling out the dough, fill a Dutch oven or heavy-bottomed pot with enough vegetable oil to cover 2 inches (5 cm). Heat the oil over low-medium heat and bring it to 350°F (180°C).

Place a wire rack over a paper towel–lined baking sheet. On a separate baking sheet, cut out thirteen 4-inch (10-cm) parchment squares for the donuts.

Roll the dough out between two pieces of well-floured parchment paper to ½ inch (1.3 cm) in thickness. Brush away any excess flour. Use well-floured 3-inch (8-cm) and 1-inch (2.5-cm) round cutters to cut out as many donuts as possible and place each on a parchment square. Reroll the dough and cut out more donuts as needed.

Use the parchment squares to gently lower two to three donuts into the hot oil. Fry the donuts for 3 minutes on the first side, then flip over and fry for 2 minutes until cooked through. Transfer the donuts to the wire rack. Wait a couple minutes for the oil to come back up to 350°F (180°C), then continue frying the donuts.

TO GLAZE: Once the donuts have cooled just enough to handle, dip them in the vanilla glaze.

Mini Powdered Sugar

Makes 28 mini donuts

You know those prepackaged mini confectioners' sugar donuts you can find at just about any gas station? As a kid, those little processed nuggets of pure sugar were my weakness on long, cross-country road trips. For the purposes of developing this recipe, I tried one again and let me tell you, they are not how I remember them. After years of making baked goods from scratch, most beloved foods from my childhood no longer appeal to my palate. And the truth of it is, nothing beats recipes made from scratch. You can still make delicious mini confectioners' sugar donuts that bring back warm, nostalgic memories, but they're made with high-quality ingredients—no additives, no preservatives—just pure donut goodness.

FOR THE DOUGH

- 300 g (2½ cups) cake flour
- 6 g (1½ tsp) baking powder
- ¼ tsp baking soda
- ½ tsp fine sea salt
- ½ tsp ground nutmeg
- 56 g (¼ cup) unsalted butter, room temperature
- 150 g (¾ cup) granulated sugar
- 1 egg, room temperature
- 1 tsp vanilla bean paste
- 170 g (¾ cup) sour cream, room temperature

FOR FRYING THE DONUTS

- 48–64 oz (1½–2 quarts) vegetable oil

TO MAKE THE DOUGH: In a large bowl, combine the flour, baking powder, baking soda, salt and nutmeg. Set it aside.

In the bowl of a stand mixer fitted with the paddle attachment, cream the butter and sugar for 2 to 3 minutes until light and fluffy. Mix in the egg and vanilla until fully combined.

Scrape down the bowl and add half of the dry ingredients. Mix on low speed until barely combined, then mix in the sour cream. Add the rest of the dry ingredients, and mix until just combined. Cover the bowl and place it in the fridge to chill for at least 1 hour or overnight.

TO FRY THE DONUTS: Just before rolling out the dough, fill a Dutch oven or heavy-bottomed pot with enough vegetable oil to cover 2 inches (5 cm). Heat the oil over low-medium heat and bring it to 350°F (180°C).

Place a wire rack over a paper towel–lined baking sheet. On a separate baking sheet, cut out twenty-eight 3-inch (8-cm) parchment squares for the donuts.

(continued)

MINI POWDERED SUGAR
(CONTINUED)

FOR THE COATING

- 227 g (2 cups) confectioners' sugar

Roll the dough out between two pieces of well-floured parchment paper to ½ inch (1.3 cm) in thickness. Brush away any excess flour. Use well-floured 2¼-inch (6-cm) and ½-inch (1.3-cm) round cutters to cut out as many donuts as possible and place each on a parchment square. Reroll the dough and cut out more donuts as needed.

Use the parchment squares to gently lower two to three donuts into the hot oil. Fry the donuts for 2 minutes on the first side, then flip over and fry for 2 minutes until golden. Transfer the donuts to the wire rack to cool completely. Wait a couple minutes for the oil to come back up to 350°F (180°C), then continue frying the donuts.

TO COAT: Once the donuts have cooled completely, quickly toss each of them in confectioners' sugar. Be careful not to handle them too much or the confectioners' sugar will melt.

DONUT BREAK

Do not underestimate the power and importance of salt in baking! The addition of salt does not make baked goods salty, but instead amplifies the flavors in the recipe. For the same reason you generously salt your water before boiling pasta, salt is added to desserts to make them more flavorful.

Not all salt is made equally! Some brands/types of salt are saltier than others and may have additives, such as anticlumping and anticaking agents. All recipes in this book were developed with pure fine sea salt. I highly recommend Celtic Sea Salt® and Redmond Real Salt®. You can also use kosher salt, such as Diamond Crystal®. Though I do not recommend using table salt, if you're in a pinch, you can substitute the sea salt for half the amount of table salt in the recipe. If in doubt about which brand to use, you can always compare the amount of sodium per ¼ teaspoon listed in the nutrition facts on the package so long as they are all the same grain size.

BRIGHT & FLORAL LEMON LAVENDER

Makes 13 donuts

There are some ingredients that seem like they belong together, and lemon and lavender are a match made in heaven. Bright citrus and calming floral flavors transform comforting old-fashioned donuts into a springtime treat that awakens your senses. While rubbing the sugar with the lemon zest and lavender buds, notice how the citrus becomes aromatic and the lavender dyes your fingertips a blueish, purple hue. The intentional infusion of these ingredients into the dough results in a complex flavor profile unlike any other. Separately, these flavors are beautiful, but together they're truly magical.

FOR THE DOUGH

- 300 g (2½ cups) cake flour
- 6 g (1½ tsp) baking powder
- ¼ tsp baking soda
- ½ tsp fine sea salt
- 150 g (¾ cup) granulated sugar
- Zest of 3 lemons
- 2 g (1 tbsp) culinary-grade lavender buds
- 56 g (¼ cup) unsalted butter, room temperature
- 1 egg, room temperature
- 1 tsp vanilla bean paste
- 170 g (¾ cup) sour cream, room temperature

FOR FRYING THE DONUTS

- 48–64 oz (1½–2 quarts) vegetable oil

TO MAKE THE DOUGH: In a large bowl, combine the flour, baking powder, baking soda and salt. Set it aside.

In a medium bowl, combine the sugar, lemon zest and lavender buds. Rub them together with your fingers until it resembles wet sand and smells aromatic.

In the bowl of a stand mixer fitted with the paddle attachment, cream the lemon-lavender sugar and butter for 2 to 3 minutes until light and fluffy. Mix in the egg and vanilla until fully combined.

Scrape down the bowl and add half of the dry ingredients. Mix on low speed until barely combined, then mix in the sour cream. Add the rest of the dry ingredients, and mix until just combined. Cover the bowl and place it in the fridge to chill for at least 1 hour or overnight.

TO FRY THE DONUTS: Just before rolling out the dough, fill a Dutch oven or heavy-bottomed pot with enough vegetable oil to cover 2 inches (5 cm). Heat the oil over low-medium heat and bring it to 350°F (180°C).

Place a wire rack over a paper towel–lined baking sheet. On a separate baking sheet, cut out thirteen 4-inch (10-cm) parchment squares for the donuts.

(continued)

BRIGHT & FLORAL LEMON LAVENDER
(CONTINUED)

FOR THE GLAZE

- 1 batch Lemon Glaze (page 143)

Meanwhile, make the lemon glaze.

Roll the dough out between two pieces of well-floured parchment paper to ½ inch (1.3 cm) in thickness. Brush away any excess flour. Use well-floured 3-inch (8-cm) and 1-inch (2.5-cm) round cutters to cut out as many donuts as possible and place each on a parchment square. Reroll the dough and cut out more donuts as needed.

Use the parchment squares to gently lower two to three donuts into the hot oil. Fry the donuts for 3 minutes on the first side, then flip over and fry for 2 minutes until golden. Transfer the donuts to the wire rack. Once they've cooled just enough to handle, dip them in the glaze. Wait a couple minutes for the oil to come back up to 350°F (180°C), then continue frying the donuts.

TO GLAZE: Once the donuts have cooled just enough to handle, dip them in the lemon glaze.

Comfy Banana Bread

Makes 11 donuts

Banana bread feels like it should always accompany comfy, cozy fall afternoons. Something about the combination of the sweet banana flavor, warm spices and moist texture feels like a warm blanket wrapped around you. Thanks to the addition of overripe bananas, these donuts have the softest, most comforting texture.

FOR THE DOUGH

- 300 g (2½ cups) cake flour
- 6 g (1½ tsp) baking powder
- ¼ tsp baking soda
- ½ tsp fine sea salt
- 4 g (2 tsp) ground cinnamon
- 56 g (¼ cup) unsalted butter, room temperature
- 106 g (½ cup, packed) dark brown sugar
- 50 g (¼ cup) granulated sugar
- 1 egg, room temperature
- 1 tsp vanilla bean paste
- 170 g (¾ cup, about 1½ medium) overripe mashed banana
- 28 g (2 tbsp) sour cream

FOR FRYING THE DONUTS

- 48–64 oz (1½–2 quarts) vegetable oil

FOR THE GLAZE

- 1 batch Cinnamon Glaze (page 143)

TO MAKE THE DOUGH: In a large bowl, combine the flour, baking powder, baking soda, salt and cinnamon. Set it aside.

In the bowl of a stand mixer fitted with the paddle attachment, cream the butter and sugars for 2 to 3 minutes until light and fluffy. Mix in the egg and vanilla until fully combined.

Scrape down the bowl and add half of the dry ingredients. Mix on low speed until barely combined, then mix in the mashed banana and sour cream. Add the rest of the dry ingredients, and mix until just combined. Cover the bowl and place it in the fridge to chill for at least 1 hour or overnight.

TO FRY THE DONUTS: Just before rolling out the dough, fill a Dutch oven or heavy-bottomed pot with enough vegetable oil to cover 2 inches (5 cm). Heat the oil over low-medium heat and bring it to 350°F (180°C).

Place a wire rack over a paper towel–lined baking sheet. On a separate baking sheet, cut out eleven 4-inch (10-cm) parchment squares for the donuts.

Roll the dough out between two pieces of well-floured parchment paper to ½ inch (1.3 cm) in thickness. Brush away any excess flour. Use well-floured 3-inch (8-cm) and 1-inch (2.5-cm) round cutters to cut out as many donuts as possible and place each on a parchment square. Reroll the dough and cut out more donuts as needed.

Use the parchment squares to gently lower two to three donuts into the hot oil. Fry the donuts for 3 minutes on the first side, then flip over and fry for 3 minutes until golden. Transfer the donuts to the wire rack. When the oil comes back up to 350°F (180°C), continue frying the donuts.

TO GLAZE: Once the donuts have cooled just enough to handle, dip them in the cinnamon glaze.

MINI PUMPKIN SPICE

Makes 28 mini donuts

I think we can all agree that pumpkin spice and the fall season are synonymous. But pumpkin spice is such a beloved flavor in the baking world, so why not make pumpkin baked goods year round? By reducing the pumpkin puree, the flavor is concentrated to come through in each and every bite.

FOR THE DOUGH

- 360 g (3 cups) cake flour
- 6 g (1½ tsp) baking powder
- ¼ tsp baking soda
- ½ tsp fine sea salt
- 6 g (1 tbsp) pumpkin pie spice
- 227 g (1 cup) reduced pumpkin puree
- 113 g (½ cup) sour cream, room temperature
- 160 g (¾ cup, packed) dark brown sugar
- 56 g (¼ cup) unsalted butter, melted
- 1 egg, room temperature
- 1 tsp vanilla bean extract

FOR FRYING THE DONUTS

- 48–64 oz (1½–2 quarts) vegetable oil

FOR THE COATING

- 1 batch Cinnamon Sugar (page 145)

TO MAKE THE DOUGH: In a large bowl, combine the flour, baking powder, baking soda, salt and pumpkin pie spice. Set it aside.

Add the pumpkin puree to a small saucepan, and place it over medium heat. Stir often with a rubber spatula until the moisture has evaporated, about 10 to 12 minutes. Weigh out 150 g (⅔ cup) of the reduced pumpkin puree in a large bowl.

Whisk in the sour cream, brown sugar, melted butter, egg and vanilla. Fold in the dry ingredients until just combined. Cover the bowl and place it in the fridge to chill for at least 1 hour or overnight.

TO FRY THE DONUTS: Just before rolling out the dough, fill a Dutch oven or heavy-bottomed pot with enough vegetable oil to cover 2 inches (5 cm). Heat the oil over low-medium heat and bring it to 350°F (180°C).

Place a wire rack over a paper towel–lined baking sheet. On a separate baking sheet, cut out twenty-eight 2-inch (5-cm) parchment squares for the donuts.

Roll the dough out between two pieces of well-floured parchment paper to ½ inch (1.3 cm) in thickness. Brush away any excess flour. Use well-floured 2¼-inch (6-cm) and ½-inch (1.3-cm) round cutters to cut out as many donuts as possible and place each on a parchment square. Reroll the dough and cut out more donuts as needed.

Use the parchment squares to gently lower three to four donuts into the hot oil. Fry the donuts for 2 minutes on the first side, then flip over and fry for 2 minutes until golden. Transfer the donuts to the wire rack. When the oil comes back up to 350°F (180°C), continue frying the donuts.

TO COAT: Once the donuts have cooled just enough to handle, toss them in the cinnamon sugar.

Spiced Apple Cider

Makes 13 donuts

When you close your eyes and take a bite of one of these spiced apple cider old-fashioned donuts, you'll wake up wearing a cozy sweater, standing in the middle of an apple orchard, with golden leaves all around you. Yes, they're that good. Made with an apple cider cake dough and covered in an apple cider glaze and cinnamon sugar coating, these donuts truly are the essence of fall!

FOR THE DOUGH

- 360 g (3 cups) cake flour
- 6 g (1½ tsp) baking powder
- ¼ tsp baking soda
- ½ tsp fine sea salt
- 1 tsp ground cinnamon
- ¼ tsp ground allspice
- ¼ tsp ground nutmeg
- 140 g (½ cup plus 1 tbsp) apple cider concentrate
- 56 g (¼ cup) unsalted butter
- 106 g (½ cup, packed) dark brown sugar
- 1 egg, cold
- 1 tsp vanilla extract
- 63 g (¼ cup) unsweetened applesauce
- 56 g (¼ cup) sour cream

FOR FRYING THE DONUTS

- 48–64 oz (1½–2 quarts) vegetable oil

TO MAKE THE DOUGH: In a large bowl, combine the flour, baking powder, baking soda, salt, cinnamon, allspice and nutmeg. Set it aside.

In a small saucepan, place the apple cider concentrate and butter over low-medium heat until the butter is fully melted. Remove the pan from the heat.

Vigorously whisk in the brown sugar until fully dissolved, then pour the mixture into a large bowl. Quickly whisk in the egg and vanilla. Then, mix in half of the dry ingredients until barely combined, followed by the applesauce and sour cream. Add in the remaining dry ingredients and gently fold with a rubber spatula until just combined. Cover the bowl and place it in the fridge to chill for at least 1 hour or overnight.

TO FRY THE DONUTS: Just before rolling out the dough, fill a Dutch oven or heavy-bottomed pot with enough vegetable oil to cover 2 inches (5 cm). Heat the oil over low-medium heat and bring it to 350°F (180°C).

Place a wire rack over a paper towel–lined baking sheet. On a separate baking sheet, cut out thirteen 4-inch (10-cm) parchment squares for the donuts.

(continued)

Spiced Apple Cider
(CONTINUED)

FOR THE COATING

- 28 g (2 tbsp) unsalted butter
- 35 g (1½ tbsp) apple cider concentrate
- 100 g (½ cup) granulated sugar
- 3 g (1½ tsp) ground cinnamon

Meanwhile, make the coating. In a small bowl, melt the butter and stir in the apple cider concentrate. Set it aside. In another medium bowl, combine the sugar and cinnamon.

Roll the dough out between two pieces of well-floured parchment paper to ½ inch (1.3 cm) in thickness. Brush away any excess flour. Use well-floured 3-inch (8-cm) and 1-inch (2.5-cm) round cutters to cut out as many donuts as possible and place each on a parchment square. Reroll the dough and cut out more donuts as needed.

Use the parchment squares to gently lower two to three donuts into the hot oil. Fry the donuts for 3 minutes on the first side, then flip over and fry for 2 minutes until golden. Transfer the donuts to the wire rack. Wait a couple minutes for the oil to come back up to 350°F (180°C), then continue frying the donuts.

TO COAT: Once the donuts have cooled just enough to handle, brush the butter-cider mixture on the top of each donut. Then, toss them in the bowl of cinnamon sugar to coat.

Zingy Ginger Molasses

Makes 14 donuts

As winter approaches, I am always eagerly awaiting molasses-flavored desserts. The sticky, sweet syrup has so much more potential than the typical gingerbread cookies. The moisture it provides baked goods makes it ideal for old-fashioned donuts, which require a careful ratio of dry to wet ingredients to ensure they maintain a soft and moist texture. But what makes molasses truly outstanding? When it's complemented by a generous amount of ginger. The ginger adds a kick, while the molasses adds warmth and the excitement of anticipating the holiday season.

FOR THE DOUGH

- 420 g (3½ cups) cake flour
- 6 g (1½ tsp) baking powder
- ¼ tsp baking soda
- ½ tsp fine sea salt
- 4 g (2 tsp) ground ginger
- 1 tsp ground cinnamon
- ¼ tsp ground cloves
- ¼ tsp ground nutmeg
- ¼ tsp ground allspice
- 170 g (½ cup) unsulfured molasses
- 56 g (¼ cup) unsalted butter, room temperature
- 106 g (½ cup, packed) dark brown sugar
- 50 g (¼ cup) granulated sugar
- 1 egg, cold
- 1 tsp vanilla bean extract
- 113 g (½ cup) sour cream, room temperature

TO MAKE THE DOUGH: In a large bowl, combine the flour, baking powder, baking soda, salt, ginger, cinnamon, cloves, nutmeg and allspice. Set it aside.

In a small saucepan, place the molasses and butter over low-medium heat until the butter is fully melted. Remove the pan from the heat.

Vigorously whisk in the sugars until fully dissolved, then pour the mixture into a large bowl. Quickly whisk in the egg and vanilla. Then, mix in half of the dry ingredients until barely combined, followed by the sour cream. Add in the remaining dry ingredients and gently fold with a rubber spatula until just combined. Cover the bowl and place it in the fridge to chill for at least 1 hour or overnight.

(continued)

Zingy Ginger Molasses
(CONTINUED)

FOR FRYING THE DONUTS

- 48–64 oz (1½–2 quarts) vegetable oil

FOR THE COATING

- Confectioners' sugar, for sprinkling

TO FRY THE DONUTS: Just before rolling out the dough, fill a Dutch oven or heavy-bottomed pot with enough vegetable oil to cover 2 inches (5 cm). Heat the oil over low-medium heat and bring it to 350°F (180°C).

Place a wire rack over a paper towel–lined baking sheet. On a separate baking sheet, cut out fourteen 4-inch (10-cm) parchment squares for the donuts.

Roll the dough out between two pieces of well-floured parchment paper to ½ inch (1.3 cm) in thickness. Brush away any excess flour. Use well-floured 3-inch (8-cm) and 1-inch (2.5-cm) round cutters to cut out as many donuts as possible and place each on a parchment square. Reroll the dough and cut out more donuts as needed.

Use the parchment squares to gently lower two to three donuts into the hot oil. Fry the donuts for 3 minutes on the first side, then flip over and fry for 3 minutes until deeply golden. Transfer the donuts to the wire rack to cool completely. Wait a couple minutes for the oil to come back up to 350°F (180°C), then continue frying the donuts.

TO COAT: Once the donuts have cooled completely, add a small amount of confectioners' sugar to a fine-mesh sieve and sprinkle it on top of the donuts.

DECADENT BAKED CAKE DONUTS

This chapter is filled with a wide variety of cake donuts with flavors ranging from ever-moist, yellow birthday cake to boozy, caramel coconut rum and to coffee-flavored coffee cake. Though the recipes vary in method, they can all be made in less than an hour! In fact, many of these recipes require just a bowl and whisk. Yes, these cake donuts are easier to make than the other recipes in this book, but make no mistake—these donuts deliver in terms of flavor, texture and appearance thanks to high-quality cake flour or unbleached all-purpose flour, large Grade AA eggs, European-style butter and high-quality, light-tasting olive oil.

INGREDIENT STAPLES

FLOUR

Depending on the recipe, you'll need either cake flour or unbleached all-purpose flour. A high-quality and common brand for cake flour is Swan's Down. Alternatively, you can make a DIY version by using all-purpose flour, taking out 15 grams (2 tbsp) and adding in 16 grams (2 tbsp) of cornstarch. For all-purpose flour, I recommend King Arthur Baking and Bob's Red Mill, or any other high-quality flour with a protein content of 10 to 12 percent.

EQUIPMENT ESSENTIALS

kitchen scale

electric mixer

donut pan

BUTTER

For optimal flavor and overall result, I recommend using a European-style butter, such as Kerrygold. European-style butters have a higher fat percentage and less water content compared to American-style butters, so they tend to have the best overall flavor and consistency for baking. After all, fat equals flavor!

It is also a general rule of thumb to use unsalted butter in order to control the total amount of salt in the recipe. You can use salted butter in any recipe, though I recommend excluding the salt listed in the recipe.

(continued)

CHEMICAL LEAVENING AGENTS

Chemical leaveners, primarily baking powder and baking soda, are essential to cake donuts' rise and texture. These leaveners lose their power over time, so if you don't bake often enough to go through them quickly, check their freshness before using. For baking powder, test a small amount in some water; and for baking soda, test a small amount in some vinegar. If they foam, you're good to go!

SOUR CREAM & YOGURT

In all recipes, sour cream and yogurt are interchangeable. I recommend baking only with plain, whole-milk Greek yogurt or a yogurt similar in consistency to Greek, such as Icelandic. The whole-milk fat content and thick consistency are ideal for best overall flavor and texture of baked goods. The same goes for sour cream in terms of fat content.

STORING DONUTS

Baked cake donuts last about 3 to 5 days stored in an airtight container at room temperature. Freeze leftover donuts in a freezer Ziploc bag for up to 3 months.

COFFEE COFFEE CAKE

Makes 12 donuts

Can we really call coffee cake coffee cake if there's no coffee in it? Sure, a sour cream cake with a gooey, cinnamon sugar swirl and buttery crumb topping would be delicious with a cup of coffee. But for my fellow coffee lovers, the coffee should really be in the cake. Thus, these coffee coffee cake donuts are made with a coffee sour cream cake, an espresso-cinnamon sugar swirl and an espresso-cinnamon crumb topping. Be sure to enjoy a donut with a cup of coffee for good measure.

FOR THE CRUMB TOPPING

- 80 g (⅔ cup) all-purpose flour
- 53 g (¼ cup, packed) dark brown sugar
- 1 tsp espresso powder
- ½ tsp ground cinnamon
- 56 g (¼ cup) unsalted butter, room temperature

FOR THE CINNAMON SUGAR SWIRL

- 20 g (1½ tbsp, packed) dark brown sugar
- 1 tsp ground cinnamon
- 1 tsp espresso powder

TO MAKE THE CRUMB TOPPING: Preheat the oven to 350°F (180°C) and grease two donut pans with butter.

In a small bowl, combine the flour, brown sugar, espresso powder and cinnamon. Cut the butter into small cubes and toss them in the mixture. Rub the mixture between your fingers until it resembles wet sand and there are no visible pieces of butter left. Cover the bowl and place it in the fridge until ready to use.

TO MAKE THE CINNAMON SUGAR SWIRL: In a small bowl, combine the brown sugar, cinnamon and espresso powder. Set it aside until ready to use.

(continued)

Coffee Coffee Cake

(CONTINUED)

FOR THE DONUTS

- 230 g (1¾ cups plus 2 tbsp) all-purpose flour
- 1 tsp baking powder
- ¼ tsp baking soda
- ½ tsp fine sea salt
- 3 g (2 tsp) espresso powder
- 85 g (6 tbsp) unsalted butter, room temperature
- 100 g (½ cup) granulated sugar
- 70 g (⅓ cup, packed) dark brown sugar
- 2 eggs, room temperature
- 1 tsp vanilla extract
- 113 g (½ cup) sour cream, room temperature
- 113 g (½ cup) freshly brewed hot coffee

FOR THE GLAZE

- ½ batch Thin Vanilla Glaze (page 143)

TO MAKE THE DONUTS: In a medium bowl, combine the flour, baking powder, baking soda, salt and espresso powder.

In the bowl of a stand mixer fitted with the paddle attachment, cream the butter and sugars for 2 to 3 minutes until light and fluffy.

Mix in the eggs and vanilla. Scrape down the bowl, then mix in half of the dry ingredients until just combined. Mix in the sour cream and hot coffee, then the remaining dry ingredients until just combined.

Spoon the batter into the prepared donut pans, filling each about one-quarter full. Sprinkle the cinnamon sugar swirl onto each, then top with more batter, filling each about three-quarters full.

Top the donuts with a generous amount of the crumb topping and bake for about 15 minutes, or until a toothpick inserted comes out clean. Allow the donuts to cool in the pan for a few minutes before transferring to a wire rack.

TO GLAZE: Make the vanilla glaze. Transfer it to a piping bag, snip the end off and pipe the glaze onto the warm donuts.

BIRTHDAY CAKE

Makes 12 donuts

Donuts were always a special birthday treat growing up, so it only seems right to make birthday cake in donut form! If you're looking for a donut fit for a celebratory occasion, you can't go wrong with a dozen of these buttery, yellow cake donuts topped with all the sprinkles. I know, I know, vanilla can be boring. But I promise, they're unlike any other yellow cake you've ever had! They have an incredibly moist, tender crumb with a balanced sweet, vanilla flavor and are topped with my Thick Vanilla Glaze (page 143).

. . . .

FOR THE DONUTS

- 180 g (1½ cups) cake flour
- 168 g (¾ cup plus 1½ tbsp) granulated sugar
- 8 g (2 tsp) baking powder
- ½ tsp fine sea salt
- 76 g (5½ tbsp) unsalted butter, room temperature
- 65 g (¼ cup plus 1 tsp) light-tasting olive oil
- 113 g (½ cup) plain whole-milk Greek yogurt, room temperature
- 113 g (½ cup) whole milk, room temperature
- 1 egg, room temperature
- 8 g (2 tsp) vanilla extract

FOR THE GLAZE + TOPPING

- 1 batch Thick Vanilla Glaze (page 143)
- Rainbow sprinkles, for topping

TO MAKE THE DONUTS: Preheat the oven to 350°F (180°C) and grease two donut pans with butter.

In the bowl of a stand mixer fitted with the paddle attachment, combine the flour, sugar, baking powder and salt.

Cut up the butter into small cubes and add them to the dry ingredients. Mix on low speed until it resembles wet sand, about 1 to 2 minutes. Add the oil, yogurt, milk, egg and vanilla. Mix until fully combined.

Spoon the batter into the prepared donut pans, filling each about three-quarters full. Bake the donuts for about 10 minutes, or until a toothpick inserted comes out clean. Allow the donuts to cool in the pan for a few minutes before transferring to a wire rack to cool completely.

TO GLAZE: Freeze the cooled donuts for 15 minutes to ensure they don't fall apart. Meanwhile, make the glaze. Dip each frozen donut into the glaze, and immediately top it with rainbow sprinkles.

MINI DOUBLE DARK CHOCOLATE

Makes 24 mini donuts

Loosely influenced by the store-bought mini chocolate covered donuts, these donuts have a snappy bittersweet chocolate coating made from the Magic Chocolate Shell Coating (page 145). The decadent flavor and fudgy texture are a result of black cocoa powder, a butter-oil combination and sour cream.

. . . .

FOR THE DONUTS

- 120 g (1 cup) cake flour
- 42 g (½ cup) Dutch process cocoa powder
- 21 g (¼ cup) black cocoa powder
- ¾ tsp baking powder
- ½ tsp fine sea salt
- 198 g (¾ cup plus 2 tbsp) unsalted butter, room temperature
- 250 g (1¼ cups) granulated sugar
- 2 eggs, room temperature
- 8 g (2 tsp) vanilla extract
- 113 g (½ cup) sour cream, room temperature
- 100 g (⅓ cup plus 1 tbsp) light-tasting olive oil

FOR THE GLAZE

- 1 batch Magic Chocolate Shell Coating (page 145)

TO MAKE THE DONUTS: Preheat the oven to 350°F (180°C) and grease one mini donut pan with butter.

In a medium bowl, combine the flour, cocoa powders, baking powder and salt. Set it aside.

In the bowl of a stand mixer fitted with the paddle attachment, cream the butter and sugar for 2 to 3 minutes until light and fluffy. Mix in the egg and vanilla. Scrape down the bowl, then mix in half of the dry ingredients until just combined. Mix in the sour cream and oil, then the remaining dry ingredients until just combined.

Spoon the batter into the prepared donut pan, filling each about two-thirds full. Bake the donuts for about 8 to 10 minutes, or until a toothpick inserted comes out clean. Allow the donuts to cool completely in the pan before removing.

TO GLAZE: Freeze the cooled donuts for 15 minutes to ensure they don't fall apart. Meanwhile, make the chocolate shell coating. Use a fork to coat each frozen donut in the chocolate and place them on a wire rack to set.

DONUT BREAK

To achieve the richest chocolate flavor, I always opt for a combination of Dutch process cocoa and black cocoa powder. Dutch process cocoa powder has a smoother flavor and creates the most fudgy and chocolatey baked goods! Black cocoa powder is similar to Dutch process, but richer in flavor and darker in color. It is typically used in small amounts alongside another cocoa powder to enhance the color and flavor of the baked good. I recommend Rodelle® Dutch process cocoa powder and King Arthur Baking black cocoa powder.

Melt-in-Your-Mouth Red Velvet

Makes 10 donuts

Red velvet seems to be one of those flavors that divides people into two categories: those who *love* it and those who are indifferent to it. I mean, no one could possibly hate it if it has cream cheese frosting on it, right?! I believe those who fall in the latter category haven't had true red velvet cake before. And what qualifies a cake as truly red velvet are four ingredients, including cocoa powder, buttermilk, white vinegar and red food coloring. These donuts take it a step further by whipping an egg white to medium peaks and folding it into the batter at the end, creating the most velvety, smooth texture.

FOR THE DONUTS

- 120 g (1 cup) all-purpose flour
- 15 g (3 tbsp) Dutch process cocoa powder
- ¼ tsp baking soda
- ½ tsp fine sea salt
- 113 g (½ cup) buttermilk, room temperature
- 1 tsp vanilla extract
- 1 tsp white vinegar
- 6 g (¾ tsp) red food gel
- 56 g (¼ cup) unsalted butter, room temperature
- 133 g (⅔ cup) granulated sugar
- 50 g (¼ cup) light-tasting olive oil
- 1 egg, separated

FOR THE GLAZE

- 1 batch Cream Cheese Glaze (page 159)

TO MAKE THE DONUTS: Preheat the oven to 350°F (180°C) and grease two donut pans with butter.

In a medium bowl, combine the flour, cocoa powder, baking soda and salt. Set it aside. In a glass measuring cup, stir the buttermilk, vanilla, vinegar and red food gel. Set it aside.

In the bowl of a stand mixer fitted with the paddle attachment, cream the butter and sugar for 2 to 3 minutes until light and fluffy. Mix in the oil and egg yolk until well combined. Add half of the dry ingredients, and mix until mostly combined. Mix in the buttermilk mixture, then the remaining dry ingredients until just combined.

In a small bowl, add the egg white and use an electric mixer to beat until medium peaks form. Using a rubber spatula, gently fold the whipped egg whites into the batter until just combined.

Spoon the batter into the prepared donut pans, filling each about three-quarters full. Bake the donuts for about 10 minutes, or until a toothpick inserted comes out clean. Allow the donuts to cool in the pan for a few minutes before transferring to a wire rack to cool completely.

TO GLAZE: Freeze the cooled donuts for 15 minutes to ensure they don't fall apart. Meanwhile, make the cream cheese glaze. Dip each frozen donut in glaze, and place it back on the wire rack to set.

DELICATE CARROT CAKE

Makes 10 donuts

I call these delicate carrot cake donuts not only to entice you to make them, but to warn you. The ever-moist crumb, albeit delicious, is reluctant to pop out of the pan in one piece. So in order to enjoy these donuts, follow the pan prep and donut removal closely! These donuts are not the same without a cream cheese glaze—more specifically, the brown butter version of this Cream Cheese Glaze (page 159).

FOR THE DONUTS

- 100 g (¾ cup plus 1 tbsp) all-purpose flour
- ¾ tsp baking powder
- ¼ tsp baking soda
- ½ tsp fine sea salt
- 1 tsp ground cinnamon
- ½ tsp ground ginger
- ¼ tsp ground nutmeg
- ¼ tsp ground allspice
- ¼ tsp ground cloves
- 65 g (¼ cup plus 1 tsp) light-tasting olive oil
- 106 g (½ cup, packed) dark brown sugar
- 32 g (2½ tbsp) granulated sugar
- 1 egg, room temperature
- 1 tsp vanilla extract
- 125 g (1¾ cups; 1–2 medium carrots) grated carrots
- 42 g (⅓ cup) pecans, finely chopped (plus more for topping, optional)

FOR THE GLAZE

- 1 batch Brown Butter–Cream Cheese Glaze (page 159)

TO MAKE THE DONUTS: Preheat the oven to 350°F (180°C). Grease two donut pans with butter and coat with flour.

In a medium bowl, combine the flour, baking powder, baking soda, salt, cinnamon, ginger, nutmeg, allspice and cloves. Set it aside.

In a separate medium bowl, whisk together the oil, sugars, egg and vanilla. Fold in the dry ingredients until mostly combined. Gently fold in the carrots and pecans until evenly distributed.

Spoon the batter into the prepared donut pans, filling each about three-quarters full. Bake the donuts for about 10 minutes, or until a toothpick inserted comes out clean.

Once the donuts are taken out of the oven, immediately use a knife to gently loosen the sides. These donuts are particularly delicate and prone to sticking to the pan: After 4 to 5 minutes—no more, no less!—loosen the sides again and promptly remove them from the pan. Then place them on a wire rack to cool completely.

TO GLAZE: Freeze the cooled donuts for 15 minutes to ensure they don't fall apart. Meanwhile, make the glaze. Dip each frozen donut in the glaze, and top it with additional pecans, if desired.

CARAMEL COCONUT RUM

Makes 11 donuts

Buttery, moist rum cake donuts coated in coconut shavings and drizzled with
a sweet rum caramel sauce are my ideal dessert. Soft cake is contrasted with
crunchy coconut, while the strong rum flavor is balanced out by rich caramel,
creating such a complex and decadent flavor profile.

FOR THE DONUTS

- 150 g (1¼ cups) all-purpose flour
- 200 g (1 cup) granulated sugar
- 5 g (1¼ tsp) baking powder
- ½ tsp fine sea salt
- 70 g (5 tbsp) unsalted butter, room temperature
- 65 g (¼ cup plus 1 tsp) light-tasting olive oil
- 90 g (⅓ cup plus 1 tbsp) unsweetened canned coconut milk
- 65 g (¼ cup plus 1 tsp) rum
- 2 eggs, room temperature
- 1 tsp vanilla extract

FOR THE SYRUP

- 36 g (3 tbsp) granulated sugar
- 21 g (1½ tbsp) unsalted butter
- 18 g (1½ tbsp) rum
- 14 g (1 tbsp) water

FOR THE COATING

- 100 g (1 cup) unsweetened shredded coconut
- ½ batch Rum Caramel Sauce (page 146)

TO MAKE THE DONUTS: Preheat the oven to 350°F (180°C) and grease two donut pans with butter.

In the bowl of a stand mixer fitted with the paddle attachment, combine the flour, sugar, baking powder and salt.

Cut up the butter into small cubes and add them to the dry ingredients. Mix on low speed until it resembles wet sand, 1 to 2 minutes. Add the oil, coconut milk, rum, eggs and vanilla. Mix until fully combined.

Spoon the batter into the prepared donut pans, filling each about three-quarters full. Bake the donuts for about 10 minutes, or until a toothpick inserted comes out clean.

While the donuts are baking, make the syrup. In a small saucepan, add the sugar, butter, rum and water. Place it over medium heat. Bring the ingredients to a boil, then turn the heat down to low and simmer for 6 minutes until the sugar has dissolved.

Remove the syrup from the heat. Allow the donuts to cool in the pan for a minute or so before transferring to a wire rack to cool just enough to handle. Brush the syrup on the warm donuts.

TO COAT: After the syrup is brushed on the donuts, immediately toss them in the coconut shavings. Make the Rum Caramel Sauce, and drizzle it on top of each donut just before serving.

Lemon Almond Olive Oil

Makes 8 donuts

If I could add extra virgin olive oil to every recipe, I would. It adds a deeper level of flavor that complements almost every dessert, especially these citrusy cake donuts. They bake up incredibly moist with a balance of flavors between the fresh lemon, almond extract and extra virgin olive oil. Bring out the lemon flavor even more with a generous coating of Lemon Glaze (page 143).

FOR THE DONUTS

- 105 g (¾ cup plus 1 tbsp) all-purpose flour
- 32 g (⅓ cup) almond flour
- ½ tsp baking powder
- ½ tsp fine sea salt
- 115 g (½ cup plus 1 tbsp) granulated sugar
- Zest of 2 lemons
- 65 g (¼ cup plus ½ tbsp) plain whole-milk Greek yogurt, room temperature
- 60 g (¼ cup) extra virgin olive oil
- 65 g (¼ cup plus 1 tsp) fresh lemon juice
- 1 egg, room temperature
- 1 tsp vanilla extract
- ½ tsp almond extract

FOR THE GLAZE

- 1 batch Lemon Glaze (page 143)

TO MAKE THE DONUTS: Preheat the oven to 325°F (165°C) and grease two donut pans with olive oil.

In a medium bowl, combine the flour, almond flour, baking powder and salt. Set it aside.

In a large bowl, add the sugar and lemon zest, and rub in between your fingers until the mixture resembles wet sand and becomes aromatic. Whisk in the yogurt, oil, lemon juice, egg and vanilla and almond extracts until fully combined. Fold in the dry ingredients until smooth.

Spoon the batter into the prepared donut pans, filling each about three-quarters full. Bake the donuts for about 10 minutes, or until a toothpick inserted comes out clean. Allow the donuts to cool in the pan for a few minutes before transferring to a wire rack to cool completely.

TO GLAZE: Freeze the cooled donuts for 15 minutes to ensure they don't fall apart. Meanwhile, make the lemon glaze. Dip each frozen donut in the glaze, and place it back on the wire rack to set.

NOSTALGIC CEREAL MILK

Makes 15 donuts

We all know the best part of eating cereal is slurping up the sugary, cereal-infused milk at the end. But maybe something you didn't know is that you can use this cereal milk to create donuts! A soft and moist cake donut infused with a childhood favorite cereal—now that's what donut dreams are made of.

FOR THE DONUTS

- 227 g (1 cup) whole milk
- 36 g (1 cup) Fruity Pebbles™ cereal
- 180 g (1½ cups) all-purpose flour
- 150 g (¾ cup) granulated sugar
- 8 g (2 tsp) baking powder
- ½ tsp fine sea salt
- 76 g (5½ tbsp) unsalted butter, room temperature
- 65 g (¼ cup plus 1 tsp) light-tasting olive oil
- 8 g (2 tsp) vanilla extract
- 2 egg whites

FOR THE COATING

- 100 g (½ cup) granulated sugar
- 18 g (½ cup) Fruity Pebbles cereal
- 28 g (2 tbsp) unsalted butter, melted

TO MAKE THE DONUTS: Preheat the oven to 350°F (180°C) and grease two donut pans with butter.

In a large glass measuring cup, combine the milk and cereal. Set it aside to infuse for about 30 minutes.

In the bowl of a stand mixer fitted with the paddle attachment, combine the flour, sugar, baking powder and salt.

Cut up the butter into small cubes and add them to the dry ingredients. Mix on low speed until it resembles wet sand, 1 to 2 minutes. Add the milk-cereal mixture, oil and vanilla. Mix until fully combined.

In a separate small bowl, use an electric mixer to whip the egg whites to medium peaks. Gently fold them into the batter with a rubber spatula until fully combined.

Spoon the batter into the prepared donut pans, filling each about three-quarters full. Bake the donuts for about 10 minutes, or until a toothpick inserted comes out clean. Allow the donuts to cool in the pan for a few minutes before transferring to a wire rack to cool completely.

TO COAT: Add the sugar and cereal to a food processor, and grind until the cereal is a fine crumb. Transfer to a medium bowl.

Brush the cooled donuts with melted butter, then toss in the sugar-cereal mixture to coat. Once all the donuts have been coated, toss them one more time for a thicker coating.

Malted Milk Chocolate

Makes 12 donuts

Chocolate cake takes on a whole new dimension of flavor with the addition of malted milk powder. By toasting the milk powder at a low temperature in the oven, the malty flavor is amplified to a level that perfectly complements the fudge-like chocolate cake. To turn these donuts into a gourmet Whoppers®-inspired dessert, cover them with the milk chocolate Magic Chocolate Shell Coating (page 145).

FOR THE DONUTS

- 140 g (1 cup) malted milk powder
- 160 g (1⅓ cups) all-purpose flour
- 125 g (½ cup plus 2 tbsp) granulated sugar
- 42 g (½ cup) Dutch process cocoa powder
- 1 tsp baking powder
- ½ tsp fine sea salt
- 150 g (⅔ cup) whole milk, room temperature
- 100 g (⅓ cup plus 1 tbsp) light-tasting olive oil
- 2 eggs, room temperature
- 1 tsp vanilla extract
- 75 g (⅓ cup) freshly brewed hot coffee, or boiling water

FOR THE GLAZE

- 1 batch Magic Chocolate Shell Coating (page 145), made with milk chocolate

TO MAKE THE DONUTS: Preheat the oven to 200°F (90°C) and line a small baking sheet with parchment paper.

Spread the malted milk powder on the baking sheet in an even layer. Bake for about 30 to 40 minutes, stirring every 10 minutes, until evenly golden. If it clumps up, pulse it in a food processor until it comes back to a fine crumb.

Once the malted milk powder has been toasted, turn the oven up to 350°F (180°C) and grease two donut pans with butter.

In a large bowl, combine the toasted malted milk powder, flour, sugar, cocoa powder, baking powder and salt. Add in the milk, oil, eggs and vanilla. Whisk until fully combined. Whisk in the hot coffee.

Spoon the batter into the prepared donut pans, filling each about three-quarters full. Bake the donuts for about 10 minutes, or until a toothpick inserted comes out clean. Allow the donuts to cool in the pan for a few minutes before transferring to a wire rack to cool completely.

TO GLAZE: Make the chocolate shell coating. Dip each donut into the chocolate, and place it back on the wire rack to set.

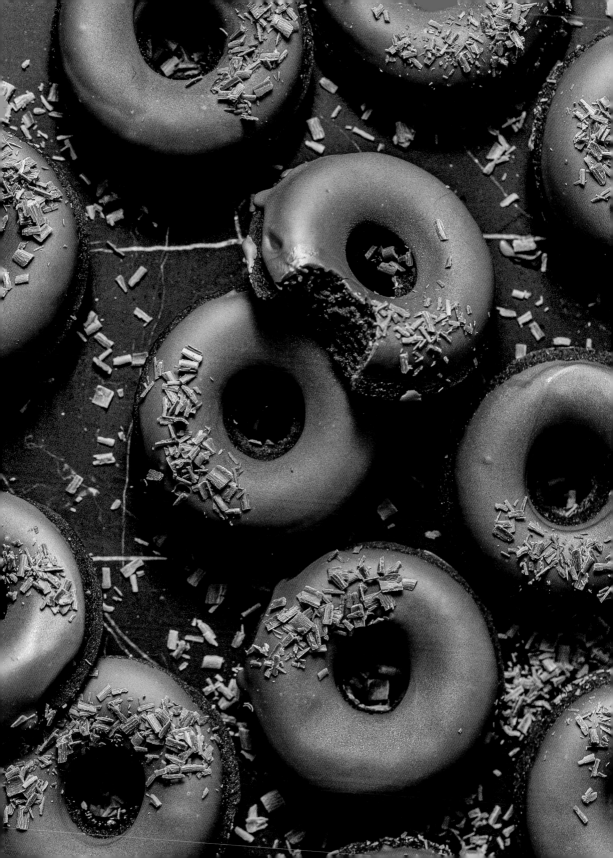

Marbled Neapolitan

Makes 12 donuts

Inspired by a childhood-favorite ice cream flavor, these donuts are made up of vanilla, chocolate and strawberry flavors marbled together. Each bite is a surprise with one flavor taking precedence over the others and changing the profile. It's almost like a game to get the perfect bite, revealing an even balance between all three flavors.

. . . .

FOR THE DONUTS

- 180 g (1½ cups) cake flour
- 168 g (¾ cup plus 1½ tbsp) granulated sugar
- 8 g (2 tsp) baking powder
- ½ tsp fine sea salt
- 76 g (5½ tbsp) unsalted butter, room temperature
- 65 g (¼ cup plus 1 tsp) light-tasting olive oil
- 227 g (1 cup) buttermilk, room temperature
- 1 egg, room temperature
- 8 g (2 tsp) vanilla extract
- 10 g (2 tbsp) Dutch process cocoa powder
- 5 g (1 tbsp) black cocoa powder
- 18 g (3 tbsp) freeze-dried strawberry powder

FOR THE GLAZE

- 1 batch Thin Vanilla Glaze (page 143)
- 5 g (1 tbsp) Dutch process cocoa powder
- 6 g (1 tbsp) freeze-dried strawberry powder

TO MAKE THE DONUTS: Preheat the oven to 350°F (180°C) and grease two donut pans with butter.

In the bowl of a stand mixer fitted with the paddle attachment, combine the flour, sugar, baking powder and salt.

Cut up the butter into small cubes and add them to the dry ingredients. Mix on low speed until it resembles wet sand, about 1 to 2 minutes. Add the oil, buttermilk, egg and vanilla. Mix until fully combined.

Divide the batter into three bowls. I recommend weighing the batter for the most accuracy. In the first bowl, mix in the cocoa powders. In the second bowl, mix in the strawberry powder. Leave the last bowl plain. Spoon a dollop of each batter into a donut cavity, and alternate the flavors until it reaches three-quarters full. Repeat with the remaining cavities; keep in mind that this recipe should make exactly twelve donuts!

Bake the donuts for about 10 minutes, or until a toothpick inserted comes out clean. Allow the donuts to cool in the pan for a few minutes before transferring to a wire rack to cool completely.

TO GLAZE: Freeze the cooled donuts for 15 minutes to ensure they don't fall apart. Meanwhile, make the vanilla glaze and divide it into three bowls. In the first bowl, mix in the Dutch process cocoa powder. In the second bowl, mix in the strawberry powder. Leave the last bowl plain.

In a large bowl, add the plain vanilla glaze. Add a few dollops of the chocolate and strawberry glazes on top, and use a toothpick or knife to swirl them together. Dip each frozen donut in the swirled glaze. Place the donuts back on the wire rack to set.

FLAKY CROISSANT DONUTS

Layers upon layers of dough and butter baked or fried to crisp, golden perfection—flaky croissant donuts are a pastry experience you do not want to miss. At first glance, you'll notice that these donuts need multiple rounds of lamination and several days of slow proofing to develop a more robust flavor. Do not be intimidated by this! If you have the time, I assure you that the technique is much simpler than you'd expect.

The Base Croissant Dough recipe (page 91) walks you through the preparation of the dough and butter block, as well as the lamination, in detail and with step-by-step photos. The individual donut recipes lay out how to shape, fry/bake, and assemble them. As a butter flavor–forward pastry with a crisp exterior, these donuts are especially delicious filled with creamy pastry cream or chocolate ganache. Their exposed flaky layers make them well suited for thick glazes piped on top or light-colored preserves brushed over the surface, making those layers shine.

INGREDIENT STAPLES

FLOUR

The quality and type of flour greatly affects the gluten development, absorption level and taste of croissant donuts. For all recipes in this chapter, I recommend an unbleached, all-purpose flour, such as King Arthur Baking and Bob's Red Mill, or any other high-quality flour with a protein content of 10 to 12 percent.

EQUIPMENT ESSENTIALS

kitchen scale   electric mixer   spider skimmer   5.5 qt dutch oven   thermometer

BUTTER

For optimal flavor and overall result, I recommend using a European-style butter, such as Kerrygold. European-style butters have a higher fat percentage and less water content compared to American-style butters, so they tend to have the best overall flavor and consistency for baking. After all, fat equals flavor!

Due to the higher fat percentage, this type of butter comes to room temperature faster and is more malleable, which is particularly important with making croissant donuts.

YEAST

For most baked goods, active dry and instant yeast are generally interchangeable. However, since the croissant dough requires a slow, multi-day proof, I recommend using active dry yeast.

STORING DONUTS

Croissant donuts are best enjoyed the day they are fried/baked. Freeze leftover donuts in a freezer Ziploc bag for up to 3 months.

Base Croissant Dough

Makes 10 to 20 donuts

Croissants are no doubt one of the most technical pastries to make, but that shouldn't be what stands between you and a buttery, flaky croissant donut. As donuts, these pastries don't need a perfect lamination technique. What they do need is a quick 1:1 flour to water poolish, which is a preferment or starter that creates a light, airy texture and stronger depth of flavor. Croissant donuts also need a three-to-four-day slow proofing process for the best overall flavor. I encourage you to follow the lamination method closely, however if you're using high-quality European-style butter, there is a very high chance that your donuts will turn out delicious no matter what. Let's face it, if there's that much butter in a recipe, it's gotta be good, right?!

FOR THE POOLISH

- 150 g (⅔ cup) water, warmed to 110°F (45°C)
- 50 g (¼ cup) granulated sugar
- 3 g (1 tsp) active dry yeast
- 150 g (1¼ cups) bread flour

FOR THE DOUGH

- 330 g (2¾ cups) all-purpose flour
- 8 g (2 tsp) fine sea salt
- 150 g (⅔ cup) whole milk, warmed to 110°F (45°C)
- 56 g (¼ cup) unsalted butter, melted

FOR THE BUTTER BLOCK

- 280 g (20 tbsp) unsalted butter, cold

DAY ONE

TO MAKE THE POOLISH: In a large bowl, combine the water, sugar, yeast and bread flour. Cover and proof in a warm environment for about 1 hour, or until doubled in size.

TO MAKE THE DOUGH: In the bowl of a stand mixer fitted with the dough hook, add the proofed poolish, all-purpose flour, salt, milk and melted butter. Mix on medium speed for about 5 minutes until smooth. Transfer the dough to a lightly greased bowl, cover and allow to proof overnight in the fridge.

TO MAKE THE BUTTER BLOCK: Fold a large piece of parchment paper into a 6-inch (15-cm) square. Cut the butter into slabs of even thickness and arrange to fit into the parchment paper. Turn the block over and use a rolling pin to gently roll the butter into a solid block. Place it in the fridge to chill overnight.

DAY TWO

TO LAMINATE: Remove the butter block from the fridge to soften at room temperature for about 30 minutes. This ensures that the butter is malleable and will roll out into one even block, resulting in more even lamination.

(continued)

BASE CROISSANT DOUGH
(CONTINUED)

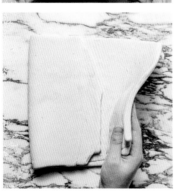

FIRST FOLD: After the butter has come to room temperature, roll the dough out on a lightly floured surface to about 8 × 14 inches (20 × 35 cm). Unwrap the butter block from the parchment paper and place it on the bottom half of the dough. Fold the top half of the dough over onto the butter block and seal the edges. Use the rolling pin to gently press horizontal indentations, then roll out to 8 × 24 inches (20 × 60 cm).

Perform a book fold, by folding the two ends up to meet each other in the middle, then fold in half (pictured below). Wrap the dough in plastic wrap, then chill it in the fridge for 30 to 45 minutes.

SECOND FOLD: After 30 to 45 minutes, roll the dough out again to 8 × 24 inches (20 × 60 cm). Perform another book fold, then wrap the dough in plastic wrap and chill it for 30 to 45 minutes.

THIRD FOLD: After 30 to 45 minutes, roll the dough out again to 8 × 24 inches (20 × 60 cm). Perform a letter fold, by folding the bottom third over the center, then top third over on top. Wrap the dough in plastic wrap and chill it overnight.

DAY THREE + DAY FOUR

Read the specific recipe directions on shaping and frying/baking.

DONUT MISS THIS

This dough can be used to make fried or baked donuts, but personally I prefer the baked method. While the fried croissant donuts have an addicting crisp texture and more classic shape, they lose their strong butter flavor due to the oil. The baked croissant donuts maintain their butter flavor, can be shaped into various forms, and don't require the hassle of deep-frying.

CREAMY DREAMY TIRAMISU

Makes 10 donuts

Contrasting textures of crisp fried croissant donuts and a creamy mascarpone filling come together to create a unique take on the elegant Italian dessert. For me, coffee-soaked, flaky croissant donuts will always win out over ladyfingers, and when topped with a generous dusting of cocoa powder? Now that's a dessert worth talking about.

FOR THE DOUGH

- 1 batch Base Croissant Dough (page 91)

FOR FRYING THE DONUTS

- 48–64 oz (1½–2 quarts) vegetable oil

DAY ONE

TO MAKE THE CROISSANT DOUGH: Follow the dough and butter block instructions as written in the Base Croissant Dough recipe (page 91).

DAY TWO

TO LAMINATE THE DOUGH: Follow the lamination instructions as written in the Base Croissant Dough recipe (page 91).

DAY THREE

TO SHAPE THE DONUTS: On a large baking sheet, cut out ten 4-inch (10-cm) parchment squares for the donuts.

On a lightly floured surface, roll the dough out to ½ inch (1.3 cm) in thickness. Brush away any excess flour. Use well-floured 3-inch (8-cm) and 1-inch (2.5-cm) round cutters to cut out as many donuts as possible and place each on a parchment square. Do not twist the cutters.

Shape the excess dough into a disk, then wrap it in plastic wrap and chill for at least 15 minutes before rerolling and cutting out more donuts.

Wrap the baking sheet well with plastic wrap and chill overnight. Alternatively, skip the overnight chill and move directly to the next step.

(continued)

CREAMY
DREAMY TIRAMISU
(CONTINUED)

FOR THE TIRAMISU FILLING

- 2 eggs, separated
- 100 g (½ cup) granulated sugar
- 227 g (1 cup) mascarpone, cold
- 56 g (¼ cup) freshly brewed coffee, cooled
- Cocoa powder, for dusting

TO ASSEMBLE THE DONUTS

Transfer the tiramisu filling to a piping bag with a medium round piping tip.

Cut the donuts in half, then brush the cooled coffee onto the inside of both halves. Pipe the tiramisu filling onto the bottom half and dust with cocoa powder. Add the top half and pipe more filling and dust with more cocoa powder. Repeat with the remaining donuts.

DONUT MISS THIS

Store the assembled leftover donuts in the fridge to keep the filling fresh.

DAY FOUR

TO FRY THE DONUTS: Remove the baking sheet from the fridge, and proof, covered, at room temperature for about 3 hours, or until nearly doubled in height.

About 30 minutes before the end of the proof time, fill a Dutch oven or heavy-bottomed pot with enough vegetable oil to cover 2 inches (5 cm). Place the oil over medium heat and bring it to 355°F (180°C). Place a wire rack over a paper towel–lined baking sheet.

Once proofed, use the parchment squares to gently lower two to three donuts into the hot oil. Fry the donuts for 2 minutes on the first side, then flip over and fry for 2 minutes until golden. Transfer the donuts to the wire rack to cool. When the oil comes back up to 355°F (180°C), continue frying the donuts. .

TO MAKE THE TIRAMISU FILLING: In a large heatproof bowl, vigorously whisk together the egg yolks and half of the sugar (50 g [¼ cup]) until the mixture is light in color and flows off the whisk. Place the bowl over a small pot of simmering water. Whisk the mixture for about 5 minutes, or until the sugar has dissolved.

Remove the bowl from the double boiler and place it in the fridge to cool for about 10 minutes. Once cool, whisk in the cold mascarpone until fully combined. Set it aside.

In a medium heatproof bowl, whisk together the egg whites and remaining sugar (50 g [¼ cup]). Place the bowl over the pot of simmering water, and whisk frequently until it reaches 120°F (49°C). Remove it from the heat and use an electric mixer to beat until stiff peaks form.

Using a rubber spatula, gently fold the meringue into the egg yolk–mascarpone mixture until just combined.

Assemble the donuts immediately (see Note).

FUNFETTI SPRINKLES & CREAM

Makes 20 donuts

Laminating rainbow sprinkles into croissant dough is such a fun way to make these donuts a little extra special. They bake up with a deep golden color, distinct flaky layers, and dots of colors inside. These playful colors and buttery flavor pair perfectly with a light and creamy Vanilla Bean Diplomat Cream (page 158). Decorate them with a Thick Vanilla Glaze (page 143) and rainbow sprinkles for a celebratory occasion!

FOR THE DOUGH

- 1 batch Base Croissant Dough (page 91)
- 76 g (⅓ cup plus 1 tbsp) rainbow sprinkles

DAY ONE

TO MAKE THE CROISSANT DOUGH: Follow the dough and butter block instructions as written in the Base Croissant Dough recipe (page 91).

DAY TWO

TO LAMINATE THE DOUGH: Follow the lamination instructions as written in the Base Croissant Dough recipe (page 91), but add half of the sprinkles to the dough just before the first book fold. Add the second half of the sprinkles to the dough just before the second book fold.

DAY THREE

TO SHAPE THE DONUTS: Line two to three baking sheets with parchment paper, and arrange twenty 3 × 1-inch (8 × 2.5-cm) tart rings spaced about 1 inch (2.5 cm) apart.

On a lightly floured surface, roll the dough out to ¼ inch (6 mm) in thickness and about 14 × 24 inches (35 × 60 cm). Using a round pastry or pizza cutter, trim the edges on the long sides, then cut ½ × 24-inch (1.3 × 60-cm) strips. Roll the strips up, careful not to let the center poke out.

(continued)

FUNFETTI SPRINKLES & CREAM
(CONTINUED)

FOR THE COATING, FILLING + TOPPING

- 1 batch Vanilla Bean Diplomat Cream (page 158)
- 1 batch Thick Vanilla Glaze (page 143)
- Rainbow sprinkles, for sprinkling

Place each roll in the tart rings. Wrap the baking sheets well with plastic wrap and chill overnight. Alternatively, skip the overnight chill and move directly to the next step.

DAY FOUR

TO BAKE THE DONUTS: Remove the baking sheets from the fridge, leave covered and proof at room temperature for about 3 hours, or until nearly doubled in height. About 30 minutes before the end of the proof time, preheat the oven to 400°F (200°C).

Place another baking sheet on top to ensure the donuts bake up with perfectly flat, golden tops. Bake for 15 minutes, then turn the oven down to 350°F (180°C) and bake for 12 minutes until deeply golden. Remove from the oven and allow the donuts to cool completely on the pan.

TO FILL: Transfer the diplomat cream to a piping bag with a very small round piping tip. Use a small paring knife to cut a wide hole in the top of each donut. Pipe the diplomat cream into each donut.

TO GLAZE: Make the vanilla glaze, and transfer to a piping bag with a very small round piping tip. Pipe the glaze onto each donut, then top them with rainbow sprinkles.

APRICOT EARL GREY

Makes 20 donuts

The combination of apricot and Earl Grey is an uncommon flavor pairing I think you'll find pleasantly surprising. I find that the sweet, yet tart, apricot preserves complement the citrusy bergamot, while balancing out the earthiness of the black tea. If you dare turn your oven on in the summer, these croissant donuts would be the perfect afternoon tea treat.

FOR THE DOUGH

- 1 batch Base Croissant Dough (page 91)

DAY ONE

TO MAKE THE CROISSANT DOUGH: Follow the dough and butter block instructions as written in the Base Croissant Dough recipe (page 91).

DAY TWO

TO LAMINATE THE DOUGH: Follow the lamination instructions as written in the Base Croissant Dough recipe (page 91).

DAY THREE

TO SHAPE THE DONUTS: Line two to three baking sheets with parchment paper, and arrange twenty 3 × 1–inch (8 × 2.5–cm) tart rings spaced about 1 inch (2.5 cm) apart. Use aluminum foil to create the center molds about 1 inch (2.5 cm) tall and ½ inch (1.3 cm) wide.

On a lightly floured surface, roll the dough out to ¼ inch (6 mm) in thickness and about 14 × 24 inches (35 × 60 cm). Using a round pastry or pizza cutter, trim the edges on the long sides, then cut ½ × 24–inch (1.3 × 60–cm) strips. Roll the strips up around the aluminum foil molds.

Place each roll in the tart rings. Wrap the baking sheets well with plastic wrap and chill overnight. Alternatively, skip the overnight chill and move directly to the next step.

(continued)

APRICOT EARL GREY
(CONTINUED)

FOR THE FILLING + GLAZE

- 1 batch Earl Grey Pastry Cream (page 158)
- Apricot preserves, for glazing

DAY FOUR

TO BAKE THE DONUTS: Remove the baking sheets from the fridge, leave covered and proof at room temperature for about 3 hours, or until nearly doubled in height. About 30 minutes before the end of the proof time, preheat the oven to 400°F (200°C).

Place another baking sheet on top to ensure the donuts bake up with perfectly flat, golden tops. Bake for 15 minutes, then turn the oven down to 350°F (180°C) and bake for 12 minutes until deeply golden. Remove from the oven and allow the donuts to cool completely on the pan.

TO FILL: Transfer the pastry cream to a piping bag with a very small round piping tip. Use a small paring knife to cut a few wide holes around the sides of each donut. Pipe the pastry cream into each donut.

TO GLAZE: Brush the apricot preserves on top of each donut.

Blood Orange Braids

Makes 8 braids

Blood oranges are one of the few citrus fruits I eagerly await all year. Their juicy flesh ranges in color from bright pink to dark purple, and it creates the most beautiful vibrant glaze. Pay close attention to how the glaze seeps into the flaky layers—it's the best part.

FOR THE DOUGH

- 1 batch Base Croissant Dough (page 91)
- Egg wash: 1 egg plus 28 g (2 tbsp) heavy cream

FOR THE COATING

- 1 batch Blood Orange Glaze (page 143)

DONUT MISS THIS

To take the guesswork out, use a stainless steel ruler for measuring the thickness and dimensions of the dough in the croissant donut recipes. You'll be amazed with how these accurate measurements minimize stress and allow you to enjoy the process more.

DAY ONE + TWO

Follow the dough and butter block and the laminating instructions as written in the Base Croissant Dough recipe (page 91).

DAY THREE

TO SHAPE THE DONUTS: Line two to three baking sheets with parchment paper. On a lightly floured surface, roll the dough out to ¼ inch (6 mm) in thickness and about 8 × 24 inches (20 × 60 cm). Using a round pastry or pizza cutter, trim the edges on the long sides, then cut 1 × 8–inch (1.3 × 20–cm) strips. Take three strips and braid them, using a few dabs of water to help the ends stick together.

Place the braids on the baking sheets spaced a few inches apart. Wrap the baking sheets well with plastic wrap and chill overnight. Alternatively, skip the overnight chill and move directly to the next step.

DAY FOUR

TO BAKE THE DONUTS: Remove the baking sheets from the fridge, leave covered and proof at room temperature for about 3 hours, or until nearly doubled in height. About 30 minutes before the end of the proof time, preheat the oven to 400°F (200°C).

Brush an egg wash onto each of the braids. Bake for 12 minutes, or until evenly golden on top, then turn the oven down to 350°F (180°C) and bake for 15 minutes until deeply golden. Remove from the oven and allow the braids to cool completely on the pan.

TO GLAZE: Make the glaze, dip each braid then place it on a wire rack to set.

WHITE CHOCOLATE CAPPUCCINO

Makes 20 donuts

Oh yes, another coffee-flavored donut—how could I resist! The highlight of this recipe truly is the filling. This espresso-infused, custard-like pastry cream might as well be ice cream, because it is worthy of being enjoyed by the spoonful. There are few things better than this luscious filling stuffed into golden, buttery croissant donuts, topped with a sweet, white chocolate ganache and a light dusting of cocoa powder.

FOR THE DOUGH

- 1 batch Base Croissant Dough (page 91)

DAY ONE

TO MAKE THE CROISSANT DOUGH: Follow the dough and butter block instructions as written in the Base Croissant Dough recipe (page 91).

DAY TWO

TO LAMINATE THE DOUGH: Follow the lamination instructions as written in the Base Croissant Dough recipe (page 91).

DAY THREE

TO SHAPE THE DONUTS: Line two to three baking sheets with parchment paper, and arrange twenty 3 × 1–inch (8 × 2.5–cm) tart rings spaced about 1 inch (2.5 cm) apart.

On a lightly floured surface, roll the dough out to ¼ inch (6 mm) in thickness and about 14 × 24 inches (35 × 60 cm). Using a round pastry or pizza cutter, trim the edges on the long sides, then cut ½ × 24–inch (1.3 × 60–cm) strips. Roll the strips up, careful not to let the center poke out.

Place each roll in the tart rings. Wrap the baking sheets well with plastic wrap and chill overnight. Alternatively, skip the overnight chill and move directly to the next step.

(continued)

White Chocolate Cappuccino

(CONTINUED)

FOR THE COATING, FILLING + TOPPING

- 1 batch Espresso Pastry Cream (page 158)
- 1 batch White Chocolate Ganache (page 144)
- Cocoa powder, for dusting

DAY FOUR

TO BAKE THE DONUTS: Remove the baking sheets from the fridge, leave covered and proof at room temperature for about 3 hours, or until nearly doubled in height. About 30 minutes before the end of the proof time, preheat the oven to 400°F (200°C).

Place another baking sheet on top to ensure the donuts bake up with perfectly flat, golden tops. Bake for 15 minutes, then turn the oven down to 350°F (180°C) and bake for 12 minutes until deeply golden. Remove from the oven and allow the donuts to cool completely on the pan.

TO FILL: Transfer the Espresso Pastry Cream to a piping bag with a very small round piping tip. Use a small paring knife to cut a wide hole in the top of each donut. Pipe the pastry cream into each donut.

TO GLAZE: Make the White Chocolate Ganache, and transfer it to a piping bag with a small round piping tip. Pipe the ganache onto each donut, then dust them with cocoa powder.

Ooey Gooey Turtle

Makes 20 donuts

After committing several days to making nearly two dozen croissant donuts, I've learned it's best to choose a filling that everyone will love. And who could say no to sweet caramel, rich chocolate and nutty pecans?! Just look at that ooey gooey pull . . .

FOR THE DOUGH

- 1 batch Base Croissant Dough (page 91)

DAY ONE

TO MAKE THE CROISSANT DOUGH: Follow the dough and butter block instructions as written in the Base Croissant Dough recipe (page 91).

DAY TWO

TO LAMINATE THE DOUGH: Follow the lamination instructions as written in the Base Croissant Dough recipe (page 91).

DAY THREE

TO SHAPE THE DONUTS: Line two to three baking sheets with parchment paper, and arrange twenty 3 × 1–inch (8 × 2.5–cm) tart rings spaced about 1 inch (2.5 cm) apart.

On a lightly floured surface, roll the dough out to ¼ inch (6 mm) in thickness and about 14 × 24 inches (35 × 60 cm). Using a round pastry or pizza cutter, trim the edges on the long sides, then cut ½ × 24–inch (1.3 × 60–cm) strips. Roll the strips up, careful not to let the center poke out.

Place each roll in the tart rings. Wrap the baking sheets well with plastic wrap and chill overnight. Alternatively, skip the overnight chill and move directly to the next step.

(continued)

Ooey Gooey Turtle
(CONTINUED)

FOR THE COATING, FILLING + TOPPING

- 100 g (¾ cup plus 2 tbsp) pecans, finely chopped
- 140 g (5 oz) semisweet or bittersweet chocolate, finely chopped
- 60 g (¼ cup) Salted Caramel Sauce (page 146)
- 1 batch Rich Chocolate Ganache (page 144)
- Pecan halves, for topping

DAY FOUR

TO BAKE THE DONUTS: Remove the baking sheets from the fridge, leave covered and proof at room temperature for about 3 hours, or until nearly doubled in height. About 30 minutes before the end of the proof time, preheat the oven to 400°F (200°C).

Place another baking sheet on top to ensure the donuts bake up with perfectly flat, golden tops. Bake for 15 minutes, then turn the oven down to 350°F (180°C) and bake for 12 minutes until deeply golden. Remove from the oven and allow the donuts to cool completely on the pan.

TO FILL: In a small bowl, combine the pecans, chocolate and caramel sauce. Transfer the turtle filling to a piping bag with a small round piping tip. Use a small paring knife to cut a wide hole in the top of each donut. Pipe the turtle filling into each donut.

TO GLAZE: Make the chocolate ganache, and transfer to a piping bag with a small round piping tip. Pipe the ganache onto each donut, then top them with a few pecan halves.

IRRESISTIBLE CHOUX DONUTS

Light and airy choux pastry is incredibly delicious with only a simple glaze, but its unique ability to fry or bake up with a hollow interior makes it optimal for any filling. Choux pastry may seem complex based on its unusual method of cooking the dough in a saucepan, but I assure you it is just as simple as making cookie dough! Pay close attention to the size and shape of the piping tip used in each recipe, as this will affect the fry/bake time as well as the yield. I find that small piping tips are best for producing crisp fried chouxnuts, and large piping tips are best for producing baked chouxnuts with extra airy, hollow interiors. As an egg-heavy pastry, choux donuts pair particularly well with strong flavors, such as chocolate or chai.

INGREDIENT STAPLES

FLOUR

Choux donuts require a bit more structural support from gluten than the rest of the donuts in this book. For all recipes in this chapter, I recommend an unbleached bread flour, such as King Arthur Baking and Bob's Red Mill, or any other high-quality flour with a protein content of 12 to 14 percent.

EQUIPMENT ESSENTIALS

kitchen scale • electric mixer • spider skimmer • 5.5 qt dutch oven • thermometer

EGGS

Since chouxnuts are a very egg-heavy pastry, it is especially important to use high-quality eggs. All recipes in this book were developed with large Grade AA eggs, weighing about 50 grams each; the size does not matter too much since the quantity for eggs is provided in grams. If you choose to add eggs based on number rather than weight, add them very slowly to the dough and pay close attention to the necessary consistency noted in the Base Choux Dough recipe (page 113).

HOW TO DISPOSE OF OIL

Frying oil cannot be poured down the sink drain. The best way to dispose of oil is to let it cool completely in the pot, then pour it back into its container and throw it away in the trash.

STORING DONUTS

Choux donuts are best enjoyed the day they are fried/baked. Freeze leftover donuts in a freezer Ziploc bag for up to 3 months.

Base Choux Dough

Makes 8 to 16 donuts

Choux is similar to brioche in the way that it is an extremely versatile dough used to create different types of pastries, from cream puffs to éclairs to choux donuts. The donut version is clearly the superior pastry, but I suppose I'm biased. You may have heard choux donuts referred to as chouxnuts or crullers, but whatever they're called, they remain the same non-yeasted pastry that smells of sugar cookies and transforms into a semi-hollow vessel perfect for any sweet or savory filling.

- 56 g (¼ cup) whole milk
- 56 g (¼ cup) water
- 56 g (¼ cup) unsalted butter
- 12 g (1 tbsp) granulated sugar
- ½ tsp fine sea salt
- 80 g (⅔ cup) bread flour
- 112 g (about 2¼) eggs, beaten
- 1 tsp vanilla bean paste

In a small saucepan, combine the milk, water, butter, sugar and salt. Place it over medium heat and bring it to a boil, or about 212°F (100°C).

Remove the saucepan from the heat. Vigorously stir in the flour with a rubber spatula until smooth and thick.

Transfer the dough to the bowl of a stand mixer fitted with a paddle attachment. Mix on low speed for about 5 minutes, or until it cools down to about 100°F (35°C).

Increase the speed to medium, and slowly stream in the eggs and the vanilla. Scrape down the bottom of the bowl and continue mixing until fully combined and smooth. To test if it's the right consistency, dip the paddle into the dough and pull up. It should form a V that breaks off after a few seconds.

Transfer the dough to a piping bag fitted with a small star tip. I recommend Ateco 864 or Wilton® 1M for thinner 2.5-inch (6-cm) fried donuts, and I use Ateco 868 or 806 for thicker 2.5-inch (6-cm) baked donuts. Furthermore, keep in mind the size of the piping tip affects the number of donuts the recipe yields.

Chill the dough for 1 hour. Meanwhile, prepare to fry or bake the choux donuts.

Classic Vanilla Bean

Makes 16 donuts

Vanilla may be written off as a plain flavor by many, but these classic vanilla bean choux donuts are anything but boring. Gorgeous flecks of vanilla bean throughout both the dough and glaze add a sweet warmth and delicate nuance. The fluted shape creates deep crevices for the glaze to settle into, creating that signature chouxnut shape.

- -

FOR THE DOUGH
- 1 batch Base Choux Dough (page 113)

FOR FRYING THE DONUTS
- 48–64 oz (1½–2 quarts) neutral oil

FOR THE GLAZE
- 1 batch Thin Vanilla Glaze (page 143)

TO FRY THE DONUTS: Fill a Dutch oven or heavy-bottomed pot with enough neutral oil to cover 2 inches (5 cm). Place the oil over medium heat and bring it to 375°F (190°C).

Place a wire rack over a paper towel–lined baking sheet. On a separate baking sheet, cut out seventeen 3-inch (8-cm) parchment squares for the donuts.

On one of the parchment squares, trace a 2½-inch (6-cm) round cutter. Place one parchment square on top, and pipe the choux dough, tracing the template. Repeat until all the dough has been piped.

Once the oil is hot enough, use the parchment squares to gently lower three to four donuts into the hot oil. The parchment will easily peel off after about 30 seconds; use tongs to remove. Fry the donuts for 90 seconds on the first side, then flip over and fry for 90 seconds until golden. Transfer the donuts to the wire rack to cool. Wait a couple minutes for the oil to come back up to 375°F (190°C), then continue frying the donuts.

TO GLAZE: Make the vanilla glaze. Once the donuts are cool enough to handle, dip each one and place it back on the wire rack to set.

DONUT BREAK

The recipes in this book use both pure vanilla extract and vanilla bean paste. They are equally potent and are interchangeable in all recipes. For recipes like vanilla glaze and vanilla pastry cream, I suggest using the paste version to show off those gorgeous vanilla bean flecks.

CHOCOLATE CHOCOLATE CREAM

Makes 8 donuts

Craquelin is essentially a cookie dough made without egg or leavening agents. When baked on top of choux pastry, it molds to the shape of the choux, and adds a contrasting texture and flavor that intrigues the senses. The way that the craquelin melts over the top of the choux and crackles as it bakes is almost as mesmerizing as seeing the perfectly hollow interior when you cut into it. Try this recipe for yourself and see how magical they truly are.

FOR THE CHOCOLATE CRAQUELIN

- 56 g (¼ cup) unsalted butter, room temperature
- 60 g (½ cup) all-purpose flour
- 5 g (1 tbsp) Dutch process cocoa powder
- 1½ tsp black cocoa powder
- 50 g (¼ cup) granulated sugar
- ½ tsp vanilla extract

FOR THE DOUGH

- 1 batch Base Choux Dough (page 113), use a large round piping tip, such as Ateco 806

FOR THE FILLING

- 1 batch Chocolate Pastry Cream (page 158)

TO MAKE THE CRAQUELIN: In the bowl of a stand mixer fitted with a paddle attachment, add the butter, flour, cocoa powders, sugar and vanilla. Mix on medium speed until a cohesive dough forms.

Roll the dough out between pieces of parchment paper to ⅛ inch (3 mm) in thickness. Freeze for at least 1 hour, or until ready to use.

TO BAKE THE DONUTS: Preheat the oven to 400°F (200°C) and line two baking sheets with parchment paper. On a separate piece of parchment paper, create a template by tracing four 4-inch (10-cm) lines.

Place the template underneath the parchment paper on one baking sheet. Pipe the choux along the lines, snipping the ends with scissors. Repeat with the second baking sheet.

Cut out eight 1 × 4-inch (2.5 × 10–cm) craquelin ovals; don't worry about making them perfect. Place one on top of each choux.

Bake the chouxnuts for 15 minutes, or until the choux no longer looks doughy, then turn the oven down to 350°F (180°C) and bake for 20 minutes until evenly golden. Allow the chouxnuts to cool completely on the baking sheet.

TO FILL: Make the Chocolate Pastry Cream and transfer to a piping bag with a large star piping tip, such as Ateco 868. Using a serrated knife, cut the top of the chouxnuts off. Pipe the chocolate pastry cream onto each and add their tops back.

RASPBERRY, ROSE & CORIANDER

Makes 16 donuts

Sweet raspberry and floral rose are a beloved flavor combination in the baking world. Though we could use just these two flavors to create a great chouxnut recipe, it really needs a spice to fully round out the flavor profile. Coriander has bright, lemony undertones and is perfect for these vibrant chouxnuts.

FOR THE DOUGH

- 56 g (¼ cup) whole milk
- 56 g (¼ cup) water
- 56 g (¼ cup) unsalted butter
- 12 g (1 tbsp) granulated sugar
- ½ tsp fine sea salt
- ½ tsp coriander
- 80 g (⅔ cup) bread flour
- 24 g (2 tbsp) freeze-dried raspberry powder
- 150 g (about 3) eggs, beaten
- 1 tsp vanilla bean paste
- ½ tsp rose water

FOR FRYING THE DONUTS

- 48–64 oz (1½–2 quarts) neutral oil

TO MAKE THE DOUGH: In a small saucepan, combine the milk, water, butter, sugar, salt and coriander. Place it over medium heat and bring it to a boil, or about 212°F (100°C).

Remove the saucepan from the heat. Vigorously stir in the flour and raspberry powder with a rubber spatula until smooth and thick.

Transfer the dough to the bowl of a stand mixer fitted with a paddle attachment. Mix on low speed for about 5 minutes, or until it cools down to about 100°F (35°C).

Increase the speed to medium, and slowly stream in the eggs, vanilla and rose water. Scrape down the bottom of the bowl and continue mixing until fully combined and smooth.

Transfer the dough to a piping bag fitted with a small star tip, such as Wilton 1M. Chill the dough for 1 hour.

TO FRY THE DONUTS: Fill a Dutch oven or heavy-bottomed pot with enough neutral oil to cover 2 inches (5 cm). Place the oil over medium heat and bring it to 375°F (190°C).

Place a wire rack over a paper towel–lined baking sheet. On a separate baking sheet, cut out seventeen 3-inch (8-cm) parchment squares for the donuts.

(continued)

RASPBERRY, ROSE & CORIANDER
(CONTINUED)

FOR THE GLAZE

- 1 batch Raspberry Rose Glaze (page 143)

On one of the parchment squares, trace a 2½-inch (6-cm) round cutter. Place one parchment square on top, and pipe the choux dough, tracing the template. Repeat until all the dough has been piped.

Once the oil is hot enough, use the parchment squares to gently lower three to four donuts into the hot oil. The parchment will easily peel off after about 30 seconds; use tongs to remove. Fry the donuts for 90 seconds on the first side, then flip over and fry for 90 seconds until golden. Transfer the donuts to the wire rack to cool. Wait a couple minutes for the oil to come back up to 375°F (190°C), then continue frying the donuts.

TO GLAZE: Make the glaze. Once the donuts are cool enough to handle, dip each one and place it back on the wire rack to set.

Chocolate Churro & Hot Chocolate

Makes 10 donuts and 1 cup of hot chocolate

A riff off the classic cinnamon sugar churros, these donuts are made with a modified base choux dough to create a chocolate choux-like dough that's fluffier with a rich chocolate flavor. To create the classic churro look, pipe the dough with a star piping tip and pair them with a decadent cup of hot chocolate.

FOR THE DOUGH

- 113 g (½ cup) water
- 28 g (2 tbsp) unsalted butter
- 12 g (1 tbsp) granulated sugar
- ¼ tsp fine sea salt
- 60 g (½ cup) bread flour
- 15 g (3 tbsp) Dutch process cocoa powder
- 1 egg, room temperature
- 1 tsp vanilla bean paste

FOR FRYING THE DONUTS

- 48–64 oz (1½–2 quarts) neutral oil

TO MAKE THE DOUGH: In a small saucepan, combine water, butter, sugar and salt. Place it over medium heat and bring it to a boil, or about 212°F (100°C).

Remove the saucepan from the heat. Vigorously stir in the flour and cocoa powder with a rubber spatula until smooth and thick.

Transfer the dough to the bowl of a stand mixer fitted with a paddle attachment. Mix on low speed for about 5 minutes, or until it cools down to about 100°F (35°C).

Increase the speed to medium, and slowly stream in the egg and the vanilla. Scrape down the bottom of the bowl and continue mixing until fully combined and smooth.

Transfer the dough to a piping bag fitted with a small star tip. I recommend Ateco 866. Chill the dough for 1 hour.

TO FRY THE DONUTS: Fill a Dutch oven or heavy-bottomed pot with enough neutral oil to cover 2 inches (5 cm). Place the oil over medium heat and bring it to 375°F (190°C).

Place a wire rack over a paper towel–lined baking sheet. On a separate baking sheet, cut out eleven 3-inch (8-cm) parchment squares for the donuts.

On one of the parchment squares, trace a 2.5-inch (6.25-cm) round cutter. Place one parchment square on top, and pipe the choux dough, tracing the template. Repeat until all the dough has been piped.

(continued)

Chocolate Churro
& Hot Chocolate
(CONTINUED)

FOR THE COATING

- 1 batch Cinnamon Sugar (page 145)

FOR THE HOT CHOCOLATE

- 113 g (½ cup) heavy cream
- 1 tsp ground cinnamon
- 113 g (4 oz) bittersweet chocolate

Once the oil is hot enough, use the parchment squares to gently lower three to four donuts into the hot oil. The parchment will easily peel off after about 30 seconds; use tongs to remove. Fry the donuts for 90 seconds on the first side, then flip over and fry for 90 seconds until crisp. Transfer the donuts to the wire rack to cool. Wait a couple minutes for the oil to come back up to 375°F (190°C), then continue frying the donuts.

TO COAT: Make the Cinnamon Sugar, and toss each donut in it to coat.

TO MAKE THE HOT CHOCOLATE: In a small saucepan, place the heavy cream and cinnamon over low-medium heat. Stir frequently with a rubber spatula and bring it to a simmer, or about 190°F (85°C).

Remove the saucepan from the heat and stir in the chocolate until fully combined and smooth. I recommend using an immersion blender to effectively combine the heavy cream and chocolate without overmixing or aggravating them.

Pour the hot chocolate into a mug or small bowl, and enjoy it with the donuts.

DIRTY CHAI CREAM

Makes 10 donuts

While fried chouxnuts have a unique texture and flavor that comes from being deep fried, baked chouxnuts have the wonderful opportunity to be coated in cookie-like craquelin. This craquelin in particular is flavored with warm chai spices, and when it is baked over the chouxnut creates a signature rippled layer. Fill these pastries with a smooth dirty chai pastry cream for maximum chai goodness.

FOR THE CHAI CRAQUELIN

- 113 g (½ cup) unsalted butter, room temperature
- 130 g (1 cup plus 1 tbsp) all-purpose flour
- 106 g (½ cup, packed) light brown sugar
- ½ tsp ground cinnamon
- ¼ tsp ground cardamom
- ¼ tsp ground ginger
- ¼ tsp ground cloves
- 1 tsp vanilla extract

FOR THE DOUGH

- 1 batch Base Choux Dough (page 113), use a large round piping tip, such as Ateco 806

FOR THE FILLING

- 1 batch Chai Pastry Cream (page 158)

TO MAKE THE CRAQUELIN: In the bowl of a stand mixer fitted with a paddle attachment, add the butter, flour, brown sugar, cinnamon, cardamom, ginger, cloves and vanilla. Mix on medium speed until a cohesive dough forms.

Roll the dough out between pieces of parchment paper to ⅛ inch (3 mm) in thickness. Freeze for at least 1 hour, or until ready to use.

TO BAKE THE DONUTS: Preheat the oven to 400°F (200°C) and line two baking sheets with parchment paper. On a separate piece of parchment paper, create a template by tracing five 2½-inch (6-cm) circles, spaced about 2 inches (5 cm) apart.

Place the template underneath the parchment paper on one baking sheet. Pipe the choux, tracing the template. Repeat with the second baking sheet.

Use 3¼-inch (8-cm) and 1¾-inch (5-cm) round cutters to cut out ten craquelin rings, and place one on top of each choux.

Bake the chouxnuts for 15 minutes, or until the choux no longer looks doughy, then turn the oven down to 350°F (180°C) and bake for 20 minutes until evenly golden. Allow the chouxnuts to cool completely on the baking sheet.

TO FILL: Make the Chai Pastry Cream and transfer to a piping bag with a large star piping tip, such as Ateco 868. Using a serrated knife, cut the top of the chouxnuts off. Pipe the chai pastry cream onto each and add their tops back.

ADDICTING SAVORY DONUTS

You may have noticed that most of the recipes in this book, aside from cake donuts, do not have a lot of sugar in the dough. For brioche, croissant and choux donuts, the sweetness comes from the fillings and glazes. So it occurred to me, why not make savory fillings and glazes?! In this chapter, you will find one savory recipe for each type of donut. Rather than serving these as an indulgent breakfast treat or dessert, savory donuts have their place as an appetizer or even served on the side of dinner, similar to a dinner roll!

EQUIPMENT ESSENTIALS

kitchen scale | electric mixer | spider skimmer | 5.5 qt dutch oven | thermometer

HOW TO DISPOSE OF OIL

Frying oil cannot be poured down the sink drain. The best way to dispose of oil is to let it cool completely in the pot, then pour it back into its container and throw it away in the trash.

STORING DONUTS

All savory donuts are best enjoyed the day they are fried/baked. Freeze leftover donuts in a freezer Ziploc bag for up to 3 months.

Garlic-Herb Brioche Knots

Makes 8 donuts

These savory brioche donuts are inspired by my ideal garlic-herb dinner roll. Every Thanksgiving, Christmas or other holiday that includes a large festive meal must have dinner rolls with copious amounts of garlic-herb butter drenched on top and a generous sprinkling of flaky sea salt. And these knots are exactly that, but uniquely shaped with a four-strand braid and fried to golden perfection.

FOR THE DOUGH

- 140 g (½ cup plus 2 tbsp) whole milk
- 1 sprig fresh rosemary
- 3 sprigs fresh thyme
- 3 fresh sage leaves
- 20 g (1½ tbsp) granulated sugar
- 7 g (2¼ tsp) instant or active dry yeast
- 2 eggs, room temperature
- 300 g (2½ cups) all-purpose flour
- 5 cloves garlic, minced
- ½ tsp fine sea salt
- 85 g (6 tbsp) unsalted butter, room temperature

TO MAKE THE DOUGH: In a small saucepan, add the milk and herbs. Place it over low heat and bring it to a simmer, stirring frequently with a rubber spatula.

Strain the milk into a glass measuring cup, then stir in the sugar and yeast. If using active dry yeast, allow it to sit for 15 minutes for the yeast to activate. If using instant yeast, simply move on to the next step.

Mix the eggs into the milk-yeast mixture.

In the bowl of a stand mixer fitted with a dough hook, mix the flour, garlic and salt. Pour the wet ingredients into the flour and mix on low-medium speed for about 3 minutes, or until it forms a ball around the hook.

Add in a few pieces of butter at a time, allowing them to fully incorporate before adding more. Once all the butter is incorporated, turn the mixer up to medium-high speed and mix for 8 to 12 minutes. The dough will eventually pull away from the sides of the bowl and have a silky-smooth texture with minimal stickiness. To check if the dough is ready, use the windowpane test: Tear off a small piece and carefully spread it out to see if you can see the light through it without it tearing.

Once the dough is ready, transfer it to a lightly greased bowl, cover and allow to proof overnight in the fridge. Alternatively, let the dough rise in a warm place for about 1 hour, or until doubled in size.

(continued)

Garlic-Herb Brioche Knots
(CONTINUED)

FOR FRYING THE DONUTS

- 48–64 oz (1½–2 quarts) neutral oil

FOR THE GARLIC-HERB BUTTER

- 56 g (¼ cup) unsalted butter
- 1 sprig fresh rosemary, finely chopped
- 1 sprig fresh thyme
- 2 fresh sage leaves, finely chopped
- 2 cloves garlic, minced
- Flaky sea salt, for sprinkling

TO FRY THE DONUTS: About 30 minutes before rolling out the dough, fill a Dutch oven or heavy-bottomed pot with enough neutral oil to cover 2 inches (5 cm). Place the oil over medium heat and bring it to 355°F (180°C).

Place a wire rack over a paper towel–lined baking sheet. On a separate baking sheet, cut out eight 4-inch (10-cm) parchment squares for the donuts.

On a lightly floured surface, roll the dough out to ¼ inch (6 mm) in thickness, about 8 × 18 inches (20 × 46 cm). Brush away any excess flour. Use a round pastry or pizza cutter to cut thirty-two ½-inch (1.3-cm) strips.

To shape the knots, take four strips and create a lattice. Starting from the top, take the strip that is underneath and bring it over across its vertical neighbor to be horizontal. Now take the horizontal strip that is underneath and bring it over its neighbor to be vertical. Repeat these steps two more times until you're back at the top, then reverse directions and repeat. Continue this pattern until the strips have run out, then tuck the ends underneath. Turn the knot over and seal the ends together.

Place each knot on a parchment square. Cover the donuts and allow them to rise for about 30 minutes, or until nearly room temperature but still slightly cool to the touch. When pressed with a finger, the dough will slowly spring back.

Once proofed, use the parchment squares to gently lower two to three donuts into the hot oil. Fry the donuts for 90 seconds on the first side, then flip over and fry for 90 seconds until golden. Transfer the donuts to the wire rack to cool. When the oil comes back up to 355°F (180°C), continue frying the donuts.

TO MAKE THE GARLIC-HERB BUTTER: In a small saucepan, add the butter, rosemary, thyme, sage and garlic. Place it over low-medium heat, stirring often until the butter has fully melted. Use a pastry brush to apply butter to each donut, then top each with flaky sea salt.

MINI CHEDDAR CHIVE CROISSANT

Makes 28 donuts

The buttery nature of croissant donuts lends them to be an ideal canvas for salty flavor profiles, namely sharp cheese. In these fried mini croissant donuts, sharp yellow Cheddar and chives are folded into the dough during the lamination process, resulting in the most addicting savory donuts.

FOR THE DOUGH

- 1 batch Base Croissant Dough (page 91)
- 227 g (2 cups) sharp Cheddar, shredded
- 5 g (2 tbsp) fresh chives

DAY ONE

TO MAKE THE CROISSANT DOUGH: Follow the dough and butter block instructions as written in the Base Croissant Dough recipe (page 91).

DAY TWO

TO LAMINATE THE DOUGH: Follow the lamination instructions as written in the Base Croissant Dough (page 91), but add half of the Cheddar and chives to the dough just before the first book fold. Add the remaining Cheddar and chives to the dough just before the second book fold.

DAY THREE

TO SHAPE THE DONUTS: On a large baking sheet, cut out twenty-eight 3-inch (8-cm) parchment squares for the donuts.

On a lightly floured surface, roll the dough out to ½ inch (1.3 cm) in thickness. Brush away any excess flour. Use well-floured 2-inch (5-cm) and ½-inch (1.3-cm) round cutters to cut out as many donuts as possible and place each on a parchment square. Do not twist the cutters.

Shape the excess dough into a disk, then wrap it in plastic wrap and chill for at least 15 minutes before rerolling and cutting out more donuts.

Wrap the baking sheet well with plastic wrap and chill overnight. Alternatively, skip the overnight chill and move directly to the next step.

(continued)

MINI CHEDDAR CHIVE CROISSANT
(CONTINUED)

FOR FRYING THE DONUTS

- 48–64 oz (1½–2 quarts) vegetable oil

DAY FOUR

TO FRY THE DONUTS: Remove the baking sheet from the fridge, leave covered and proof at room temperature for about 3 hours, or until nearly doubled in height.

About 30 minutes before the end of the proof time, fill a Dutch oven or heavy-bottomed pot with enough vegetable oil to cover 2 inches (5 cm). Place the oil over medium heat and bring it to 355°F (180°C).

Place a wire rack over a paper towel–lined baking sheet.

Once proofed, use the parchment squares to gently lower three to four donuts into the hot oil. Fry the donuts for 2 minutes on the first side, then flip over and fry for 2 minutes until golden. Transfer the donuts to the wire rack to cool. Wait a couple minutes for the oil to come back up to 355°F (180°C), then continue frying the donuts.

Mini Honey-Corn Bread Old-Fashioned

Makes 20 donuts

Everyone seems to have an opinion on corn bread, but I always prefer a sweet corn bread with a dense, slightly coarse texture. And that's exactly what these savory old-fashioned donuts are. Their miniature size and light drizzling of honey makes them perfect for dipping into a warm bowl of chili.

FOR THE DOUGH

- 180 g (1½ cups) all-purpose flour
- 140 g (1 cup plus 2 tbsp) cornmeal, medium grind
- 6 g (1½ tsp) baking powder
- ¼ tsp baking soda
- ½ tsp fine sea salt
- 56 g (¼ cup) unsalted butter, melted
- 50 g (¼ cup) light-tasting olive oil
- 50 g (¼ cup) granulated sugar
- 26 g (2 tbsp, packed) light brown sugar
- 1 egg, room temperature
- 113 g (½ cup) sour cream, room temperature

FOR FRYING THE DONUTS

- 48–64 oz (1½–2 quarts) vegetable oil

FOR THE GLAZE

- Honey, for drizzling

TO MAKE THE DOUGH: In a medium bowl, combine the flour, cornmeal, baking powder, baking soda and salt. Set it aside.

In a large bowl, whisk together the butter, oil, sugars and egg until fully combined. Whisk in half of the dry ingredients, then the sour cream. Fold in the remaining dry ingredients until fully combined. Cover the bowl and place it in the fridge to chill for at least 1 hour or overnight.

TO FRY THE DONUTS: Just before rolling out the dough, fill a Dutch oven or heavy-bottomed pot with enough vegetable oil to cover 2 inches (5 cm). Heat the oil over low-medium heat and bring it to 350°F (180°C).

Place a wire rack over a paper towel–lined baking sheet. On a separate baking sheet, cut out twenty 3-inch (8-cm) parchment squares for the donuts.

Roll the dough out between two pieces of well-floured parchment paper to ½ inch (1.3 cm) in thickness. Brush away any excess flour.

Use well-floured 2¼-inch (6-cm) and ½-inch (1.3-cm) round cutters to cut out as many donuts as possible and place each on a parchment square. Reroll the dough and cut out more donuts as needed.

Use the parchment squares to gently lower two to three donuts into the hot oil. Fry the donuts for 2 minutes on the first side, then flip over and fry for 2 minutes until golden. Transfer the donuts to the wire rack to cool. When the oil comes back up to 350°F (180°C), continue frying the donuts.

TO GLAZE: Drizzle honey over the warm donuts.

Baked Asiago Zucchini

Makes 12 donuts

Imagine an Asiago bagel-zucchini bread mashup with an Italian spice twist. Now add a crunchy sharp cheese topping contrasted with a warm, soft interior, and you have these unique baked Asiago zucchini donuts. There is so much flavor in such an unassuming type of donut!

FOR THE DONUTS

- 240 g (2 cups) all-purpose flour
- 1 tsp baking powder
- ½ tsp baking soda
- 1 tsp fine sea salt
- 1 tsp dried oregano
- ½ tsp cracked fennel seed
- ½ tsp crushed red chiles
- ½ tsp garlic powder
- 100 g (⅓ cup plus 1 tbsp) extra virgin olive oil
- 113 g (½ cup) plain whole-milk Greek yogurt, room temperature
- 2 eggs, room temperature
- 150 g (1 cup, about 1 medium) grated zucchini
- 113 g (1¼ cup) grated aged Asiago cheese, plus more for topping

TO MAKE THE DONUTS: Preheat the oven to 350°F (180°C) and grease two donut pans with olive oil.

In a medium bowl, combine the flour, baking powder, baking soda, salt, oregano, fennel seed, crushed red chiles and garlic powder. Set it aside.

In a large bowl, vigorously whisk together the oil, yogurt and eggs until fully combined. Fold in the dry ingredients until mostly combined. At this point, the batter will be very thick. Fold in the zucchini and Asiago until evenly dispersed.

Spoon the batter into the prepared donut pans, filling each about three-quarters full. Bake the donuts for about 10 minutes, or until a toothpick inserted comes out clean. Allow the donuts to cool completely in the pan.

Transfer the baked donuts to a large baking sheet and top them with extra Asiago. Place on the top rack in the oven, then broil on high for about 5 minutes until the cheese melts and becomes crisp.

SPINACH ARTICHOKE CHOUX

Makes 10 donuts

The filling in these savory chouxnuts is a unique take on spinach artichoke dip. One taste of this gorgeous green, creamy filling will have you scrambling to make another batch.

FOR THE DOUGH

- 1 batch Base Choux Dough (page 113), remove sugar and vanilla; use Ateco 864

FOR FRYING THE DONUTS

- 48–64 oz (1½–2 quarts) neutral oil

FOR THE SPINACH ARTICHOKE FILLING

- 6 g (1½ tsp) extra virgin olive oil
- 25 g shallot, diced
- 1 clove garlic, minced
- 113 g (4 oz) cream cheese
- 56 g (¼ cup) plain whole-milk Greek yogurt
- 56 g (½ cup) grated Parmesan
- 56 g (½ cup) mozzarella
- 100 g (3.5 oz) marinated artichoke hearts, roughly chopped
- 30 g (1 cup) raw spinach

FOR THE COATING (OPTIONAL)

- 28 g (¼ cup) grated Parmesan

TO FRY THE DONUTS: Fill a Dutch oven or heavy-bottomed pot with enough neutral oil to cover 2 inches (5 cm). Place the oil over medium heat and bring it to 375°F (190°C).

Place a wire rack over a paper towel–lined baking sheet. On a separate baking sheet, cut out eleven 3-inch (8-cm) parchment squares for the donuts. On one of the parchment squares, trace a 2½-inch (6-cm) round cutter. Place one parchment square on top, and pipe the choux dough, tracing the template. Repeat until all the dough has been piped.

Once the oil is hot enough, use the parchment squares to gently lower three to four donuts into the hot oil. The parchment will easily peel off after about 30 seconds; use tongs to remove. Fry the donuts for 90 seconds on the first side, then flip over and fry for 90 seconds until golden. Transfer the donuts to the wire rack to cool. When the oil comes back up to 375°F (190°C), continue frying the donuts.

TO MAKE THE FILLING: In a medium saucepan, add the oil and place it over medium heat. Add the shallot, stirring frequently until translucent. Stir in the garlic, then turn the heat down to low. Add in the cream cheese, yogurt, Parmesan, mozzarella, artichoke and spinach, stirring often until the cheeses have melted and the spinach has wilted slightly.

Remove the pan from the heat. Use an immersion blender or transfer the mixture to a blender, and blend until smooth. Transfer the filling to a piping bag with a small round piping tip.

TO FILL: Turn the cooled donuts over and poke a few holes in the bottom with a toothpick, big enough for the piping tip. Pipe the spinach artichoke filling into each donut. Sprinkle Parmesan on top, if desired.

TEMPTING GLAZES, FILLINGS & TOPPINGS

This chapter is filled with base recipes for various glazes, fillings and toppings, with numerous options to switch up the flavors. Sometimes a craving hits for a classic glazed donut, and other times a donut needs to be dressed up a little with a fun glaze and filling. Whether you're looking for a basic thin vanilla glaze for a simple glazed brioche donut from The Classic Trio (page 15) or a creamy, floral Earl Grey pastry cream for these Apricot Earl Grey croissant donuts (page 99), you'll be able to customize these base recipes to suit all of your donut moods.

EQUIPMENT ESSENTIALS

kitchen scale   saucepan   immersion blender

Simple Vanilla Glaze

Makes enough for 13 donuts

FOR THE THIN VANILLA GLAZE

- 170 g (1 ½ cups) confectioners' sugar
- 113 g (½ cup) heavy cream
- 1 ½ tsp vanilla bean paste or extract

FOR THE THICK VANILLA GLAZE

- 227 g (2 cups) confectioners' sugar
- 28 g (2 tbsp) plain whole-milk Greek yogurt or sour cream
- 84 g (¼ cup plus 2 tbsp) heavy cream
- ½ tsp vanilla bean paste or extract

In a small bowl, whisk together all the ingredients until smooth.

RECIPE VARIATIONS

ESPRESSO: In the thick vanilla glaze, replace the heavy cream with 28 to 42 grams (2 to 3 tbsp) of freshly brewed espresso, depending on desired thickness.

LEMON: In the thin glaze, replace the heavy cream with 36 grams (3 tbsp) of fresh squeezed lemon juice.

CINNAMON: In either glaze, add ½ teaspoon of ground cinnamon.

BLOOD ORANGE: In the thick glaze, replace the yogurt and heavy cream for 50 grams (¼ cup) of fresh squeezed blood orange juice.

RASPBERRY ROSE: In the thin glaze, add 6 grams (1 ½ tsp) of freeze-dried raspberry powder and ¼ teaspoon of rose water.

Rich Chocolate Ganache

Makes enough for 12 donuts or 16 mini donuts

- 113 g (½ cup) heavy cream
- 113 g (4 oz) bittersweet or semisweet chocolate, roughly chopped

In a small saucepan, place the heavy cream over low-medium heat. Stir frequently with a rubber spatula and bring it to a simmer, or about 190°F (85°C).

Remove the pan from the heat and add the chocolate. Use an immersion blender to blend until smooth. Alternatively, you can use a rubber spatula to gently combine them. However, I highly recommend using an immersion blender, as it effectively combines the heavy cream and chocolate without overmixing or aggravating them.

Recipe Variations

MOCHA: Simmer the heavy cream with 3 grams (2 tsp) of espresso powder. Continue the recipe as written above.

WHITE CHOCOLATE: Replace the chocolate with 113 grams (4 oz) of white chocolate, and reduce the heavy cream to 56 grams (¼ cup). Heat the white chocolate and heavy cream in a small bowl over a pot of simmering water until fully melted. Remove the bowl from the heat and allow it to cool for 15 minutes. Mix in 56 grams (½ cup) of confectioners' sugar.

Cinnamon Sugar

Makes enough for 13 donuts or 28 mini donuts

- 100 g (½ cup) granulated sugar
- 3 g (1 ½ tsp) ground cinnamon

In a small shallow bowl, combine the sugar and cinnamon.

For best results, toss donuts warm from the deep fryer as soon as they're cool enough to touch.

Recipe Variation

Espresso: Add 1 teaspoon of espresso powder.

Magic Chocolate Shell Coating

Makes enough for 12 donuts or 24 mini donuts

- 340 g (12 oz) bittersweet, semisweet or milk chocolate

Finely chop half of the chocolate. Set it aside.

Roughly chop the remaining half of the chocolate and add it to a small heatproof bowl. Place it over a small saucepan of simmering water. Stir the chocolate frequently until fully melted and smooth.

Turn the heat off. With the bowl still on top of the saucepan, gently stir in the chocolate until smooth. Use immediately for coating donuts.

Recipe Variation

White Chocolate: Use 340 grams (12 oz) of white chocolate; follow the instructions as written above.

Salted Caramel Sauce

Makes enough for 13 donuts

- 200 g (1 cup) granulated sugar
- ½ tsp fine sea salt
- ¼ tsp cream of tartar
- 30 g (2 tbsp) water
- 113 g (½ cup) heavy cream, room temperature
- 84 g (6 tbsp) unsalted butter, room temperature
- 1 tsp vanilla bean paste
- Pinch of flaky sea salt

In a small saucepan, combine the sugar, salt, cream of tartar and water. Place it over medium-high heat, stirring often with a rubber spatula to encourage even cooking.

When it comes to a boil, reduce the heat to medium and continue stirring often. After about 10 minutes, when the color turns an even medium amber color, slowly stream in the heavy cream, quickly mixing until fully combined. Then, mix in the butter and vanilla. Once the butter has melted, continue cooking and stirring with the rubber spatula for 1 minute.

Remove the caramel from the heat and pour it into a glass jar. Stir in a pinch or two of flaky sea salt. Chill in the fridge overnight, or until ready to use.

Recipe Variations

BROWN BUTTER: Replace the room temperature unsalted butter with 86 grams (6 tbsp) melted and cooled brown butter.

To make the brown butter, start with 113 grams (½ cup) of unsalted butter. Add the butter to a small saucepan—light in color so you can see clearly! Place it over medium heat. As the butter melts, mix with a rubber spatula to encourage even cooking. Once the butter has fully melted, it will alternate between rapid large bubbles and gentle small foamy bubbles.

The butter will be ready once it turns a dark golden color and the fat solids have darkened and settled at the bottom of the pan. Immediately pour it into a medium bowl, scraping out the fat solids at the bottom, and weigh out to 86 grams (6 tbsp). Allow it to cool to room temperature, and continue the caramel sauce recipe as written above.

RUM: Stir in 12 grams (1 tbsp) of rum at the end with the butter and vanilla.

SILKY MERINGUE

Makes enough for 13 donuts

- 70 g (about 2) egg whites
- 100 g (½ cup) granulated sugar
- ¼ tsp fine sea salt
- ½ tsp vanilla bean paste

In a medium heatproof bowl, whisk together the egg whites, sugar and salt. Place the bowl over a small saucepan of simmering water, whisking the mixture frequently until it reaches 160°F (70°C) or the sugar is completely dissolved and the egg whites do not feel grainy.

Using an electric mixer, beat on high speed until soft peaks form, then add the vanilla. Continue mixing until stiff peaks form. Use the meringue to decorate the donuts immediately.

WHIPPED CREAM

Makes enough for 12 donuts

- 113 g (½ cup) heavy cream
- 12 g (1 tbsp) granulated sugar
- ½ tsp vanilla bean paste or extract

In a small bowl or glass measuring cup, combine the heavy cream, sugar and vanilla. Use an electric mixer to beat until soft peaks form. Check the consistency often to avoid over-whipping the cream.

TART LEMON CURD

Makes enough for 13 donuts

- 132 g (⅔ cup) granulated sugar
- Zest of 2 lemons
- 8 g (1 tbsp) cornstarch
- ½ tsp fine sea salt
- 42 g (3 tbsp) unsalted butter
- 4 egg yolks
- 132 g (½ cup plus 1 tbsp) fresh squeezed lemon juice

In a medium bowl, add the sugar and lemon zest. Rub them together with your fingers until it resembles wet sand and smells aromatic. Whisk in the cornstarch and salt. Set it aside.

In a small saucepan, melt the butter over low-medium heat. Whisk in the sugar mixture, then the egg yolks and lemon juice. Use a rubber spatula to constantly mix for about 10 minutes, or until large bubbles form. Immediately remove it from the heat.

Strain the lemon curd through a fine-mesh sieve into a medium bowl. Cover the bowl and chill overnight.

RECIPE VARIATION

ORANGE: Replace the lemon juice with an equal amount of fresh squeezed orange juice. Use any type of orange, such as navel, blood or Cara Cara.

DONUT MISS THIS

Save your egg whites and make Silky Meringue (page 149) for a full lemon meringue situation.

SALTED CARAMEL POPCORN

Makes 6 cups

- 20 g (1½ tbsp) olive oil
- 80 g (⅓ cup plus 1 tbsp) corn kernels
- 106 g (½ cup, packed) light brown sugar
- 56 g (¼ cup) salted butter
- 56 g (¼ cup) heavy cream
- 1½ tsp fine sea salt
- 1 tsp vanilla extract

Preheat the oven to 250°F (120°C) and line a large baking sheet with parchment paper.

In a large pot, add the oil and corn kernels. Place it over medium heat and cover with a tight lid. The kernels will start popping after a few minutes. Once popping slows, check to make sure most of the kernels have popped, then place the lid back on and remove it from the heat.

While the popcorn is popping, make the caramel. In a medium saucepan, combine the sugar, butter, heavy cream and salt. Place it over medium heat and bring it to a boil, stirring frequently. Continue boiling until it reaches 250°F (120°C). Remove it from the heat and stir in the vanilla. Allow it to cool for a few minutes.

Remove one heaping cup of the popcorn and set it aside. Spread the rest of the popcorn on the prepared baking sheet. Pour the caramel on top and use a rubber spatula or your hands to gently mix until evenly coated.

Spread the popcorn back in an even layer, then bake for 30 minutes, stirring every 10 minutes.

Once the popcorn comes out of the oven, mix in the reserved plain popcorn. Allow to set for about 15 minutes, then break apart.

Fluffy Vanilla Bean Marshmallows

Makes 81 1-inch (2.5-cm) marshmallows

- 226 g (1 cup) water, divided
- 16 g (2 packets) unflavored gelatin powder
- 400 g (2 cups) granulated sugar
- 170 g (⅔ cup) light corn syrup
- 1 tsp fine sea salt
- 12 g (1 tbsp) vanilla bean paste
- Confectioners' sugar, for dusting

Line a 9-inch (23-cm) square pan with parchment paper. Liberally grease the parchment paper with softened butter and sprinkle with confectioners' sugar.

In the bowl of a stand mixer fitted with a whisk attachment, add the first 113 grams (½ cup) of water and sprinkle the gelatin on top in an even layer. Set it aside to bloom.

In a small saucepan, combine the other 113 grams (½ cup) of water, sugar, light corn syrup and salt. Heat the saucepan over medium heat, stirring frequently until the sugar dissolves. Raise the heat to medium-high, and without stirring, bring it to 240°F (115°C).

While the mixer is on low speed, slowly drizzle the hot sugar over the gelatin. Once all the hot sugar is poured in, increase the mixer speed to high and mix until thick and cool, about 100°F (40°C). Add the vanilla while it is mixing.

Pour the marshmallow mixture into the prepared pan. Tap the pan on the counter a few times to release any air bubbles. Loosely cover, and allow to set at room temperature for at least 4 hours or overnight.

Once set, turn the marshmallow mixture out onto a surface liberally dusted with confectioners' sugar. Sprinkle more confectioners' sugar on top, then cut into 1-inch (2.5-cm) squares, and toss the marshmallows together in a bowl of confectioners' sugar.

VANILLA BEAN PASTRY CREAM

Makes enough for 12 donuts or 20 mini donuts

- 227 g (1 cup) whole milk
- 4 egg yolks
- 100 g (½ cup) granulated sugar
- 16 g (2 tbsp) cornstarch
- 28 g (2 tbsp) unsalted butter
- 1 tsp vanilla bean paste

In a small saucepan, place the milk over low-medium heat and bring it to a simmer or about 190°F (85°C).

Meanwhile, in a medium bowl, vigorously whisk together the egg yolks, sugar and cornstarch until pale in color and the mixture flows off the whisk.

Once the milk has reached a simmer, slowly pour half of it into the egg-sugar mixture while simultaneously whisking to temper the eggs. Pour everything back into the saucepan and place it over medium heat. Use a rubber spatula to mix constantly as it thickens.

Once the pastry cream is thick and a few big bubbles come to the surface, continue whisking for 1 minute, then remove the pan from the heat.

Immediately add the butter and vanilla, and use an immersion blender or rubber spatula to combine. Pour the pastry cream through a fine-mesh sieve into a small bowl to ensure it's perfectly smooth.

Press plastic wrap up against the surface of the pastry cream to prevent a skin from forming. Place it in the fridge to chill overnight, or until ready to use.

Once ready to use, whisk the pastry cream until it becomes a smooth, pipeable consistency.

VANILLA BEAN PASTRY CREAM
(CONTINUED)

RECIPE VARIATIONS

STRAWBERRY: In a small saucepan, combine 85 grams (½ cup) of hulled and quartered fresh strawberries, 18 grams (3 tbsp) of freeze-dried strawberry powder, 50 grams (¼ cup) of sugar and 56 grams (¼ cup) of water. Place it over medium heat, stirring frequently for 10 to 12 minutes until the strawberries have broken down.

Use an immersion blender or transfer to a blender, and blend until smooth. Pour 227 grams (1 cup) of milk into the syrup and mix to combine.

Weigh 227 grams (1 cup) of the strawberry milk out for the pastry cream and pour the remainder into a glass jar. Continue the recipe as written.

CREAM CHEESE: After the pastry cream has chilled overnight—Add 113 grams (4 oz) of cold block-style cream cheese to the pastry cream, and whisk until smooth.

DIPLOMAT: After the pastry cream has chilled overnight—In a small bowl, add 113 grams (½ cup) of cold heavy cream. Use an electric mixer to whip the cream to medium peaks. Using a rubber spatula, fold the whipped cream into the whisked pastry cream until fully combined. Use immediately.

ESPRESSO: Add 10 grams (1 tbsp) of espresso to the milk, then bring it to a simmer. Continue the recipe as written.

EARL GREY: Bring the milk to a boil or 212°F (100°C), rather than a simmer, then remove it from the heat and steep 15 grams (3 tbsp) of loose-leaf Earl Grey tea for about 10 minutes. Strain the milk into another saucepan, weighing it out once more to ensure it's still at 227 grams (1 cup); add more milk if needed. Bring the Earl Grey milk back to a simmer or 190°F (85°C) and continue the recipe as written.

CHOCOLATE: Add in 113 grams (4 oz) of bittersweet or semisweet chocolate with the butter and vanilla.

CHAI: Bring the milk to a boil or 212°F (100°C), rather than a simmer, then remove it from the heat and steep 12 grams (2 tbsp) of loose-leaf chai for about 10 minutes. Strain the milk into another saucepan, weighing it out once more to ensure it's still at 227 grams (1 cup); add more milk if needed. Bring the chai milk back to a simmer or 190°F (85°C) and continue the recipe as written.

Cream Cheese Glaze

Makes enough for 10 donuts

- 56 g (¼ cup) unsalted butter, melted
- 113 g (4 oz) cream cheese, room temperature
- 170 g (1½ cups) confectioners' sugar, sifted
- 28 g (2 tbsp) heavy cream

In a medium bowl, vigorously whisk the melted butter and cream cheese until fully combined and smooth.

Add the sifted confectioners' sugar a little at a time, whisking between each addition. Once all the confectioners' sugar is added, mix in the heavy cream until smooth.

Recipe Variation

BROWN BUTTER: Replace the 56 grams (¼ cup) of melted unsalted butter with 56 grams (¼ cup) of melted brown butter.

To make the brown butter, start with 70 g (5 tbsp) of unsalted butter. Add the butter to a small saucepan—light in color so you can see clearly! Place it over medium heat. As the butter melts, mix with a rubber spatula to encourage even cooking. Once the butter has fully melted, it will alternate between rapid large bubbles and gentle small foamy bubbles.

The butter will be ready once it turns a dark golden color and the fat solids have darkened and settled at the bottom of the pan. Immediately pour into a medium bowl, scraping out the fat solids at the bottom, and weigh out to 56 grams (¼ cup). Continue the glaze recipe as written above.

ACKNOWLEDGMENTS

The process of bringing this cookbook to life was truly a team effort. I would be remiss if I did not conclude with a heartfelt thank you to all who made this book possible.

To the team at Page Street Publishing: Thank you for making my dream a reality. I am forever grateful for the opportunity to create a tangible book I can call my own. Aïcha and Marissa, both of you have been so wonderful to work with, and I am so appreciative of all that you have done to produce the best possible version of my work.

To Noah, my favorite person: I could not have done this without your unwavering support and encouragement. Thank you for being my dedicated taste tester, for enduring late-night photo shoots, and for accepting the never-ending stockpile of donuts flooding our tiny box of an apartment.

To my family: Thank you for your patience and understanding as I committed myself to such an unusual career path. Everything you have done for me is appreciated more than you will ever know.

To my friends, both near and far, who frequently checked in on me and encouraged me to come up for air every now and then. Your friendship means the world to me.

Last, thank you to the readers of Sloane's Table, as well as those of you who have just stumbled upon this book, for re-creating my recipes in your own kitchens. Every like, comment, share, message, blog visit and review does not go unnoticed. Your support is the reason I get to live out my dream every day, and I am endlessly grateful for this.

ABOUT THE AUTHOR

Sloane Papa is a recipe developer, food photographer and the creator of Sloane's Table. Sloane's work has been featured in *Half & Half* magazine. She has also partnered with *Bake from Scratch* magazine and renowned food brands, including Bob's Red Mill™, Valrhona™ and Red Star Yeast™. She lives in New York City where she bakes and creates content in her tiny studio apartment.

INDEX

A

advance preparation, 20

almond extract/flour, in Lemon Almond Olive Oil, 80

Apple Cider, Spiced, 59–60

apples, in Boozy Bourbon Apple Fritters, 21–22

Apricot Earl Grey, 99–100

artichoke hearts, in Spinach Artichoke Choux, 139

asiago cheese, in Baked Asiago Zucchini, 136

B

Baked Asiago Zucchini, 136

baking powder/soda, 43

bananas, in Comfy Banana Bread, 55

Base Brioche Donut Dough, 13–14

Base Choux Dough, 113

Base Croissant Dough, 91–92

Birthday Cake, 71

black cocoa powder

about, 72

Chocolate Chocolate Cream, 117

Chocolate Sour Cream, 46

Marbled Neapolitan, 87

Mini Double Dark Chocolate, 72

Blood Orange Braids, 103

Blood Orange Glaze

recipe, 143

Blood Orange Braids, 103

Bomboloni, Nutella, 40

Boozy Bourbon Apple Fritters, 21–22

Boston Cream, Mini, 26

bourbon

Boozy Bourbon Apple Fritters, 21–22

bourbon glaze, 22

braided donuts

Blood Orange Braids, 103

Coffee Coffee Coffee, 29–30

Garlic-Herb Brioche Knots, 129–130

Bright & Floral Lemon Lavender, 51–52

brioche donuts

about, 11

baking, 14

Base Brioche Donut Dough, 13–14

Boozy Bourbon Apple Fritters, 21–22

classic chocolate sprinkle, 15–16

classic cinnamon sugar, 15–16

The Classic Trio, 15–16

Coffee Coffee Coffee, 29–30

Cozy Hot Chocolate, 39

Garlic-Herb Brioche Knots, 129–130

glazed donut, 15–16

Lemon Meringue, 36

Mini Boston Cream, 26

Mini Strawberry & Cardamom, 31–32

Nutella Bomboloni, 40

proofing the dough, 11, 14

Raspberry Cheesecake, 35

Strawberries & Cream, 19–20

The Ultimate Caramel Movie Snack, 25

Brown Butter Caramel Sauce

recipe, 146

The Ultimate Caramel Movie Snack, 25

Brown Butter-Cream Cheese Glaze

recipe, 159

Delicate Carrot Cake, 76

butter, 11, 89

C

cake donuts, baked

about, 65–66

Baked Asiago Zucchini, 136

Birthday Cake, 71

Caramel Coconut Rum, 79

Coffee Coffee Cake, 67–68

Delicate Carrot Cake, 76

Lemon Almond Olive Oil, 80

Malted Milk Chocolate, 84

Marbled Neapolitan, 87

Melt-in-Your-Mouth Red Velvet, 75

Mini Double Dark Chocolate, 72

Nostalgic Cereal Milk, 83

cake donuts, fried

about, 43

Bright & Floral Lemon Lavender, 51–52

Chocolate Sour Cream, 46

Classic Sour Cream, 45

Comfy Banana Bread, 55

Mini Honey-Corn Bread Old-Fashioned, 135

Mini Powdered Sugar, 49–50

Mini Pumpkin Spice, 56

Spiced Apple Cider, 59–60

Zingy Ginger Molasses, 61–62

caramel
  Brown Butter Caramel Sauce, 146
  Caramel Coconut Rum, 79
  Ooey Gooey Turtle, 107–109
  Rum Caramel Sauce, 146
  Salted Caramel Popcorn, 153
  Salted Caramel Sauce, 146
  The Ultimate Caramel Movie Snack, 25

cardamom, in Mini Strawberry & Cardamom, 31–32

carrots, in Delicate Carrot Cake, 76

cereal, in Nostalgic Cereal Milk, 83

chai craquelin, 125

Chai Pastry Cream
  recipe, 157–158
  Dirty Chai Cream (donut), 125

chai spices, in Dirty Chai Cream (donut), 125

cheese
  Baked Asiago Zucchini, 136
  Brown Butter-Cream Cheese Glaze, 159
  cream cheese and vanilla bean pastry cream, 157–158
  Cream Cheese Glaze, 159
  Creamy Dreamy Tiramisu, 93–94
  Delicate Carrot Cake, 76
  Melt-in-Your-Mouth Red Velvet, 75
  Mini Cheddar Chive Croissant, 131–132
  Raspberry Cheesecake, 35
  Spinach Artichoke Choux, 139

chemical leaveners, 43

chives, in Mini Cheddar Chive Croissant, 131–132

chocolate
  Chocolate Chocolate Cream, 117

Chocolate Churro & Hot Chocolate, 121–122

chocolate craquelin, 117

Chocolate Pastry Cream, 157–158

Chocolate Sour Cream, 46

classic chocolate sprinkle, 15–16

cocoa powders, 72

Cozy Hot Chocolate, 39

Magic Chocolate Shell Coating, 145

Malted Milk Chocolate, 84

Marbled Neapolitan, 87

Mini Boston Cream, 26

Mini Double Dark Chocolate, 72

Ooey Gooey Turtle, 107–109

Rich Chocolate Ganache, 144

See also white chocolate

Chocolate Ganache, Rich
  recipe, 144
  classic chocolate sprinkle, 15–16
  Cozy Hot Chocolate, 39
  Mini Boston Cream, 26
  Ooey Gooey Turtle, 107–109

chocolate hazelnut spread, in Nutella Bomboloni, 40

Chocolate Pastry Cream
  recipe, 157–158
  Chocolate Chocolate Cream, 117

choux donuts
  about, 111
  Base Choux Dough, 113
  Chocolate Chocolate Cream, 117
  Chocolate Churro & Hot Chocolate, 121–122
  Classic Vanilla Bean, 114
  Dirty Chai Cream, 125

Raspberry, Rose & Coriander, 118–120

Spinach Artichoke Choux, 139

churro, in Chocolate Churro & Hot Chocolate, 121–122

Cinnamon Glaze
  recipe, 143
  Comfy Banana Bread, 55

Cinnamon Sugar
  recipe, 145
  Chocolate Churro & Hot Chocolate, 121–122
  classic cinnamon sugar donut, 15–16
  Mini Pumpkin Spice, 56

cinnamon sugar swirl
  recipe, 67
  Coffee Coffee Cake, 67–68

Classic Sour Cream, 45

Classic Trio, The, 15–16

Classic Vanilla Bean, 114

cocoa powder
  about, 72
  Chocolate Chocolate Cream, 117
  Chocolate Churro & Hot Chocolate, 121–122
  Chocolate Sour Cream, 46
  Malted Milk Chocolate, 84
  Marbled Neapolitan, 87
  Melt-in-Your-Mouth Red Velvet, 75
  Mini Double Dark Chocolate, 72

coconut, in Caramel Coconut Rum, 79

coffee
  Coffee Coffee Cake, 67–68
  Coffee Coffee Coffee, 29–30
  Creamy Dreamy Tiramisu, 93–94
  espresso-cinnamon crumb topping, 67

Espresso-Cinnamon Sugar, 67, 145

Espresso Pastry Cream, 157–158

Espresso Swirled Glaze, 143

Malted Milk Chocolate, 84

Mocha Ganache, 144

White Chocolate Cappuccino, 104–106

Comfy Banana Bread, 55

confectioners' sugar

    Mini Powdered Sugar, 49–50

    Zingy Ginger Molasses, 61–62

coriander, in Raspberry, Rose & Coriander, 118–120

cornmeal, in Mini Honey-Corn Bread Old-Fashioned, 135

Cozy Hot Chocolate, 39

craquelins

    for Chocolate Chocolate Cream, 117

    for Dirty Chai Cream (donut), 125

cream cheese, in Brown Butter-Cream Cheese Glaze

    recipe, 159

    Delicate Carrot Cake, 76

Cream Cheese Glaze

    recipe, 159

    Melt-in-Your-Mouth Red Velvet, 75

Cream Cheese Pastry Cream

    recipe, 157–158

    Raspberry Cheesecake, 35

Creamy Dreamy Tiramisu, 93–94

croissant donuts

    about, 89, 103

    Apricot Earl Grey, 99–100

    Base Croissant Dough, 91–92

    Blood Orange Braids, 103

    Creamy Dreamy Tiramisu, 93–94

Funfetti Sprinkles & Cream, 97–98

Mini Cheddar Chive Croissant, 131–132

Ooey Gooey Turtle, 107–109

White Chocolate Cappuccino, 104–106

crullers. See choux donuts

crumb topping, 67

curd, orange, 150

Curd, Tart Lemon

    recipe, 150

    Lemon Meringue (donut), 36

D

Delicate Carrot Cake, 76

Diplomat Cream, Vanilla Bean

    recipe, 157–158

    Funfetti Sprinkles & Cream, 97–98

Dirty Chai Cream, 125

donut recipes, and advance preparation, 20

Dutch process cocoa powder

    about, 72

    Chocolate Chocolate Cream, 117

    Chocolate Churro & Hot Chocolate, 121–122

    Chocolate Sour Cream, 46

    Malted Milk Chocolate, 84

    Marbled Neapolitan, 87

    Melt-in-Your-Mouth Red Velvet, 75

    Mini Double Dark Chocolate, 72

E

Earl Grey tea

    Apricot Earl Grey, 99–100

    Earl Grey Pastry Cream, 157–158

eggs, 111

espresso-cinnamon crumb topping, 67

Espresso-Cinnamon Sugar

    recipes, 67, 145

    Coffee Coffee Coffee, 29–30

Espresso Pastry Cream

    recipe, 157–158

    White Chocolate Cappuccino, 104–106

Espresso Swirled Glaze

    recipe, 143

    Coffee Coffee Coffee, 29–30

F

filled donuts

    Apricot Earl Grey, 99–100

    Chocolate Chocolate Cream, 117

    Cozy Hot Chocolate, 39

    Creamy Dreamy Tiramisu, 93–94

    Dirty Chai Cream, 125

    Funfetti Sprinkles & Cream, 97–98

    Lemon Meringue, 36

    Mini Boston Cream, 26

    Nutella Bomboloni, 40

    Ooey Gooey Turtle, 107–109

    Raspberry Cheesecake, 35

    Spinach Artichoke Choux, 139

    Strawberries & Cream, 19–20

    White Chocolate Cappuccino, 104–106

fillings

    about, 141

    Chai Pastry Cream, 157–158

    Earl Grey Pastry Cream, 157–158

    Tart Lemon Curd, 150

    Tiramisu filling, 94

    Vanilla Bean Diplomat Cream, 157–158

    Vanilla Bean Pastry Cream, 157–158

    Whipped Cream, 149

flour
    for baked cake donuts, 65–66
    for brioche donuts, 11
    for choux donuts, 111
    for croissant donuts, 89
    for fried cake donuts, 43
Fluffy Vanilla Bean Marshmallows
    recipe, 154
    Cozy Hot Chocolate, 39
Fritters, Boozy Bourbon Apple, 21–22
Fruity Pebbles cereal, in Nostalgic Cereal Milk, 83
Funfetti Sprinkles & Cream, 97–98

G

Ganache, Mocha
    recipe, 144
    Coffee Coffee Coffee, 29–30
Ganache, Rich Chocolate
    recipe, 144
    classic chocolate sprinkle, 15–16
    Cozy Hot Chocolate, 39
    Mini Boston Cream, 26
    Ooey Gooey Turtle, 107–109
Ganache, White Chocolate
    recipe, 144
    White Chocolate Cappuccino, 104–106
Garlic-Herb Brioche Knots, 129–130
ginger, in Zingy Ginger Molasses, 61–62
glazed donuts
    Apricot Earl Grey, 99–100
    Birthday Cake, 71
    Blood Orange Braids, 103
    Boozy Bourbon Apple Fritters, 21–22
    Bright & Floral Lemon Lavender, 51–52
    Chocolate Sour Cream, 46

classic chocolate sprinkle, 15–16
classic glazed, 15–16
Classic Sour Cream, 45
Classic Vanilla Bean, 114
Coffee Coffee Cake, 67–68
Coffee Coffee Coffee, 29–30
Comfy Banana Bread, 55
Delicate Carrot Cake, 76
Funfetti Sprinkles & Cream, 97–98
Lemon Almond Olive Oil, 80
Malted Milk Chocolate, 84
Marbled Neapolitan, 87
Melt-in-Your-Mouth Red Velvet, 75
Mini Boston Cream, 26
Mini Double Dark Chocolate, 72
Mini Honey-Corn Bread Old-Fashioned, 135
Ooey Gooey Turtle, 107–109
Raspberry, Rose & Coriander, 118–120
The Ultimate Caramel Movie Snack, 25
White Chocolate Cappuccino, 104–106
glazes
    about, 141
    Blood Orange Glaze, 143
    bourbon glaze, 22
    Brown Butter-Cream Cheese Glaze, 159
    Cinnamon Glaze, 143
    Cream Cheese Glaze, 159
    Espresso Swirled Glaze, 143
    Lemon Glaze, 143
    Magic Chocolate Shell Coating, 145
    Raspberry Rose Glaze, 143
    Rich Chocolate Ganache, 144
    Simple Vanilla Glaze, 143

H

herbs, in Garlic-Herb Brioche Knots, 129–130
honey, in Mini Honey-Corn Bread Old-Fashioned, 135

L

lavender, in Bright & Floral Lemon Lavender, 51–52
leaveners, 11, 43
Lemon Almond Olive Oil, 80
Lemon Curd, Tart
    recipe, 150
    Lemon Meringue (donut), 36
Lemon Glaze
    recipe, 143
    Bright & Floral Lemon Lavender, 51–52
    Lemon Almond Olive Oil, 80
Lemon Meringue (donut), 36

M

Magic Chocolate Shell Coating
    recipe, 145
    Malted Milk Chocolate, 84
    Mini Double Dark Chocolate, 72
Malted Milk Chocolate, 84
Marbled Neapolitan, 87
Marshmallows, Fluffy Vanilla Bean
    recipe, 154
    Cozy Hot Chocolate, 39
mascarpone, in Creamy Dreamy Tiramisu, 93–94
Melt-in-Your-Mouth Red Velvet, 75
Meringue, Silky
    recipe, 149
    Lemon Meringue (donut), 36
Mini Boston Cream, 26
Mini Cheddar Chive Croissant, 131–132
Mini Double Dark Chocolate, 72
Mini Honey–Corn Bread Old-Fashioned, 135
Mini Powdered Sugar, 49–50
Mini Pumpkin Spice, 56

Mini Strawberry & Cardamom, 31–32

Mocha Ganache
    recipe, 144
        Coffee Coffee Coffee, 29–30

molasses, in Zingy Ginger Molasses, 61–62

N

Neapolitan, Marbled, 87

Nostalgic Cereal Milk, 83

Nutella Bomboloni, 40

O

oil, disposing of, 11

old-fashioned donuts
    about, 43
        Bright & Floral Lemon Lavender, 51–52
        Chocolate Sour Cream, 46
        Classic Sour Cream, 45
        Comfy Banana Bread, 55
        Mini Honey-Corn Bread Old-Fashioned, 135
        Mini Powdered Sugar, 49–50
        Mini Pumpkin Spice, 56
        Spiced Apple Cider, 59–60
        Zingy Ginger Molasses, 61–62

olive oil, in Lemon Almond Olive Oil, 80

Ooey Gooey Turtle, 107–109

orange juice/zest
        Blood Orange Braids, 103
        Blood Orange Glaze, 143
        Nutella Bomboloni, 40
        orange curd, 150

P

Pastry Cream, Vanilla Bean
    recipe, 157–158
        Mini Boston Cream, 26

pecans
        Delicate Carrot Cake, 76
        Ooey Gooey Turtle, 107–109

poolish, 91

Popcorn, Salted Caramel
    recipe, 153
        The Ultimate Caramel Movie Snack, 25

Powdered Sugar, Mini, 49–50

preparation, in advance, 20

proofing brioche dough, 11

pumpkin, in Mini Pumpkin Spice, 56

R

Raspberry, Rose & Coriander, 118–120

Raspberry Cheesecake, 35

Raspberry Rose Glaze
    recipe, 143
        Raspberry, Rose & Coriander, 118–120

recipes, and advance preparation, 20

Red Velvet, Melt-in-Your-Mouth, 75

Rich Chocolate Ganache
    recipe, 144
        classic chocolate sprinkle, 15–16
        Cozy Hot Chocolate, 39
        Mini Boston Cream, 26
        Ooey Gooey Turtle, 107–109

rose water
        Raspberry, Rose & Coriander, 118–120
        Raspberry Rose Glaze, 143

rosemary, in Garlic-Herb Brioche Knots, 129–130

Rum Caramel Sauce
    recipe, 146
        Caramel Coconut Rum, 79

S

sage, in Garlic-Herb Brioche Knots, 129–130

salt, 50

Salted Caramel Popcorn
    recipe, 153
        The Ultimate Caramel Movie Snack, 25

Salted Caramel Sauce
    recipe, 146
        Ooey Gooey Turtle, 107–109

savory donuts
    about, 127
        Baked Asiago Zucchini, 136
        Garlic-Herb Brioche Knots, 129–130
        Mini Cheddar Chive Croissant, 131–132
        Mini Honey-Corn Bread Old-Fashioned, 135
        Spinach Artichoke Choux, 139

Silky Meringue
    recipe, 149
        Lemon Meringue (donut), 36

Simple Vanilla Glaze, 143

sour cream
    about, 43
        Chocolate Sour Cream, 46
        Classic Sour Cream, 45

Spiced Apple Cider, 59–60

Spinach Artichoke Choux, 139

Strawberries & Cream, 19–20

Strawberry & Cardamom, Mini, 31–32

Strawberry Pastry Cream
    recipe, 157–158
        Strawberries & Cream, 19–20

strawberry powder, in Marbled Neapolitan, 87

T

Tart Lemon Curd
    recipe, 150
        Lemon Meringue (donut), 36

Thick Vanilla Glaze
    recipe, 143
        Birthday Cake, 71
        Funfetti Sprinkles & Cream, 97–98

Thin Vanilla Glaze
    recipe, 143

Chocolate Sour Cream, 46

classic glazed donut, 15–16

Classic Sour Cream, 45

Classic Vanilla Bean, 114

Coffee Coffee Cake, 67–68

Marbled Neapolitan, 87

thyme, in Garlic-Herb Brioche Knots, 129–130

Tiramisu, Creamy Dreamy, 93–94

toppings

    about, 141

    chai craquelin, 125

    chocolate craquelin, 117

    Cinnamon Sugar, 145

    cinnamon sugar swirl, 67

    crumb topping, 67

    Fluffy Vanilla Bean Marshmallows, 154

    Mocha Ganache, 144

    Rich Chocolate Ganache, 144

    Salted Caramel Popcorn, 153

    Silky Meringue, 149

    Whipped Cream, 149

    White Chocolate Ganache, 144

    See also glazes

U

Ultimate Caramel Movie Snack, The, 25

V

Vanilla Bean, Classic, 114

Vanilla Bean Diplomat Cream

    recipe, 157–158

    Funfetti Sprinkles & Cream, 97–98

Vanilla Bean Marshmallows, Fluffy

    recipe, 154

    Cozy Hot Chocolate, 39

Vanilla Bean Pastry Cream

    recipe, 157–158

    Mini Boston Cream, 26

Vanilla Glaze, Thick

    recipe, 143

    Birthday Cake, 71

    Funfetti Sprinkles & Cream, 97–98

Vanilla Glaze, Thin

    recipe, 143

    Chocolate Sour Cream, 46

    classic glazed donut, 15–16

    Classic Sour Cream, 45

    Classic Vanilla Bean, 114

    Coffee Coffee Cake, 67–68

    Marbled Neapolitan, 87

W

Whipped Cream

    recipe, 149

    Strawberries & Cream, 19–20

White Chocolate Cappuccino, 104–106

White Chocolate Ganache

    recipe, 144

    White Chocolate Cappuccino, 104–106

white chocolate shell coating, 145

windowpane test, 14

Y

yeast, 11, 89

yeast donuts

    Base Brioche Donut Dough, 13–14

    Base Croissant Dough, 91–92

    Boozy Bourbon Apple Fritters, 21–22

    classic chocolate sprinkle, 15–16

    classic cinnamon sugar, 15–16

    classic glazed, 15–16

    The Classic Trio, 15–16

    Coffee Coffee Coffee, 29–30

    Cozy Hot Chocolate, 39

    Garlic-Herb Brioche Knots, 129–130

    Lemon Meringue, 36

    Mini Boston Cream, 26

    Mini Strawberry & Cardamom, 31–32

    Nutella Bomboloni, 40

    Raspberry Cheesecake, 35

    Strawberries & Cream, 19–20

    The Ultimate Caramel Movie Snack, 25

yogurt, 43

Z

Zingy Ginger Molasses, 61–62

zucchini, in Baked Asiago Zucchini, 136